M000187301

POVERTY
CURSE
BROKEN

The Roberta Hoskie Story

R O B E R T A   H O S K I E

Trilogy Christian Publishers A Wholly Owned Subsidary of Trinity Broadcasting Network 2442 Michelle Drive Tustin, CA 92780

Copyright © 2019 by Roberta Hoskie

All rights reserved, including the right to reproduce this book or portions thereof in any form whatsoever. For information, address Trilogy Christian Publishing Rights Department, 2442 Michelle Drive, Tustin, Ca 92780.

For information about special discounts for bulk purchases, please contact Trilogy Christian Publishing.

Manufactured in the United States of America

10 9 8 7 6 5 4 3 2 1

Library of Congress Cataloging-in-Publication Data is available.

ISBN 978-1-64088-255-3 (Paperback)
ISBN 978-1-64088-256-0 (ebook)

This book is dedicated to my Children; Dante, Oliver, Allia, my unborn grandchildren, and great-grandchildren. May you forever know that "You're Destined for Greatness".

If you hear the dogs, keep going.
If you see the torches in the woods, keep going.
If there's shouting after you, keep going.
Don't ever stop. Keep going.
If you want a taste of freedom, keep going.

—Harriet Tubman

Acknowledgments

I WOULD LIKE TO FIRST, thank God for keeping me through the struggles of my life and bringing me to the other side. Thank you to my family, especially to my Children, for being my "Why" in life. Thank you to Cheryl Robinson, who encouraged me to write my story and reminded me that only I could take the pen to write the story of my life.

Contents

The book, The Poverty Curse Broken, discusses how God brought one woman—Roberta Hoskie—from poverty to prosperity. It is an emotional autobiography of the life chronicles of Dr. Roberta A. Hoskie.

Prologue

I FOUND MYSELF PREGNANT AT seventeen, in an abusive relationship, a high school dropout, on welfare, and homeless. Growing up in the inner city of New Haven, Connecticut, I was exposed to abuse, crime, and poverty at a very young age. My first boyfriend, Trayvon, was killed by a close-range gunshot wound to his chest as he left my house one evening around 8:00 pm. Subsequently, I began to hang out in the streets with other young people from the local gang.

Quickly, I found myself in the wrong place at the wrong time. I was sitting in the back seat of a parked car, behind the driver's seat on the corner of Edgewood Avenue and Orchard Street. Suddenly, gunfire broke out from a passing car; purposely shooting up the car where I was a passenger. The driver was shot in the arm, the front seat passenger was shot in the chest, and the person in the back seat, next to me, was shot in the leg. I was the only person in the car untouched by the bullets that were clearly meant to assassinate all of the passengers. This situation made me seriously think about life in the hood.

While thinking of my past and the violence in it, I gave birth to my "brown baby boy" and reality smacked me in the face. I was now responsible for raising a "black man" in today's society. This was a scary place for me once I realized that I had nothing to offer my son—except a life of poverty and everything that comes along with such a life.

I was a high school dropout, and his father was a drug dealer, who was hoping to avoid a jail sentence. The statistics were not in my favor and definitely not in my son's favor. I knew that the statistics meant I would either lose my son to the streets, to the jail cell, or worse—his life to gang violence.

The power of a mother's love was exemplified when I would stop at absolutely nothing to better myself so that I could provide a better life for my child. I desperately wanted to hold on to prophecies that were given to me as a little girl by my godparents, who were both pastors. They told me that I was "destined for greatness" and that "God was going to make my name great, and He would use me to help so many people." They also told me to focus on life and keep pushing until the prophecies became a reality.

After years of struggle, I ultimately invested in a real estate transaction that yielded me over a quarter of a million dollars. My life was drastically transformed, and this was the beginning of my journey from "poverty to prosperity".

Why I Decided to Write This Book

As I SAT ON MY balcony in Myrtle Beach, South Carolina at 2 a.m. watching the waters, after a storm that just passed, I felt an extreme calmness and a sense of clarity about this book.

It is absolutely necessary that you apply the techniques in this book and the steps at the end of the book if you want the wretched curse of poverty to be removed from you and your family. Poverty is a generational curse. Many of you have accepted poverty as a lifestyle; yet, it is not the Maker's design. It is clearly a trick of the enemy to have you settle and become complacent with such a life.

The truth is that poverty is a spirit, a mindset, and a curse that can and will be broken if you follow the rules of engagement that is outlined in this book. I know what poverty is because I come from a long line of poverty-stricken family members from both my paternal and maternal sides of my family. At one point in my life, I recall twenty-two family members all living in the same low-income housing complex—all at the same time!

THE GENERATIONAL CURSE

My great-grandmother had a child as a teenager, my grandmother had a child as a teenager, my mother had a child as a teenager, my sister had a child as a teenager, and I had a child as a teenager. This cycle is not a coincidence, but rather it is a generational curse to birth a lifetime of poverty. And those are some deep family roots. So, I made up my mind as a teenager that this curse would stop with me, and the curse would not be passed on to my children. At the time, I didn't quite understand poverty, and I didn't understand spiritual curses. I didn't know how I was going to do it, but I knew that somehow it had to be done.

I vividly remember the day I made up my mind that poverty was not for me. I was sixteen years old and standing in the kitchen of my godparents' home in North Branford, CT. They had recently, picked me up from a homeless teenage shelter. My godparents, Robert and Cynthia Pulley, are pastors of Outreach for Christ Ministries in Virginia Beach, VA.

My godmother looked me deep in my eyes and said, "God has a plan for you; know that you can do anything you put your mind to and in faith, you can accomplish that thing." She also said, "…and Baby, you don't have to be a product of your environment."

Her words ricocheted within my spirit. It was something about the words she had spoken and how they had ignited something deep down in my spirit. Up until then, I had never known that I had a choice, but on that particular day, I realized that I did. I looked her directly in the eyes, and I said, "When I make it out of the ghetto, I am not ever coming back." I meant those words with all of my heart, and previously, I had never spoken with such authority or with such definite purpose.

So, I decided right then and there that whatever it took to live the life I so desperately dreamed of having, I would do whatever was necessary; no matter what it took. However, I was still a child, and life hadn't totally hit me, yet. My godfather told me that I was a "dreamer". He had nicknamed me Josephine, the female version of Joseph, the dreamer in the Bible.

A dreamer, yes, that's me. However, over the years, I learned that dreams are precursors to phenomenal life-changing successes. The Acronym that I like to use for D.R.E.A.M. is Divinely Revealed Events Awaiting Manifestation.

So, I encourage everyone who reads this book to dream. Dream without boundaries because if you can see it in your mind, then you can live it in your life. Dream because God is showing you what he has in store for you. Dream because that is who you are destined to become, especially, when you break the curse of poverty. Notice that I did not say "if" you break the curse of poverty, but I said, "when" you break the curse of poverty. It is your destiny!

I encourage you to take the time to evaluate your life. Are you where you desire to be in life? If the answer is no then keep reading this book.

Chapter One

I HEARD THE GUNSHOTS, I jumped out of my bed and ran into my son's room as fast as I could. My heart was beating so fast that I didn't have time to think. I quickly grabbed my baby, pulled him to the cold floor, and I laid my entire body over him—to keep him out of harm's way. There was gunfire exploding right outside of my son's bedroom window. I was so scared for his life that mine didn't matter. My son wasn't going to end up like the little girl, who one week prior, had lost her life to a stray bullet while she sat innocently in her stroller.

Father, help us, we can't live like this, I thought.

I have to make it out of the hood because our lives depended on it. Crime was everywhere, and innocent people were falling victims. The world seemed to be so cruel and so unfair. Survival was the name of the game.

So, here I am with this little brown boy, who didn't ask to be born to a high school dropout. Who didn't ask to be poverty plagued. Who didn't ask for a welfare recipient mother with nothing to offer him except a world of big problems and little hope. Obviously, the statistics were clearly stacked up against my brown boy. But what statistics, society and people underestimated was the *power of a mother's love.*

Yes, we definitely had the statistics to show that poverty would be perpetual in my bloodline. But when the Creator of the entire universe has a plan for your life, then all of the statistics in the world do not matter.

Crime, violence, murder, homelessness, anger, bitterness, and resentment was all too common in my everyday life. I remember, my first love, he was a lady's man—light complexion, soft curly hair, and a smile that would brighten anyone's day. He would look me in my eyes and tell me how much he loved me and yes, as a fifteen-year-old, I believed him. Being a naïve teenager, I believed every word out of his mouth.

He had a mellow demeanor with a bit of mystery about himself. From the start, I knew he was a hustler. He sold drugs in the public housing projects on Church Street South, which we used to call the "Jungle" and yes, the name said it all. A real jungle—it had prostitutes, drug addicts, crackheads, baseheads, and of course, the drug dealers. They all hung out in the Jungle. Hip Hop music from Big Daddy Kane, Wu-Tang Clan, A Tribe Called Quest, and Public Enemy was played loudly from a ragtop, Candy Apple Red Volvo with the custom Gucci Seats as it drove slowly through the hood and would stop to check in with "my man". I should have felt nervous in this environment, but instead, I felt right at home. Pat, my best friend at the time, was dating his cousin, so we spent a lot of time hanging out in the Jungle with our guys.

Although Trayvon was a hustler, he was also a huge family-oriented person. He loved his mother and his siblings. He would do anything for them. In fact, he confided in me, the first and the only time I went fishing was with his father and his siblings, that he hustled to be able to provide for his family. There was something so sobering and calming about fishing. We were in the woods with orange, burgundy, and yellow leaves all around us. It was a very scenic view as the river flowed, and I heard the water splashing on the rocks.

"I caught one!" Trayvon said as he wrestled with the fishing rod and finally pulled in his six-inch fish. We all laughed because of the way he was fighting with the fishing rod; we thought he had at least a six-footer! I believe it was this kind funny part of him, which I focused on that allowed me to override the bad boy in him.

Trayvon would call it protective, others would call it jealousy, and my mother just called it insane behavior. "I climbed on top of the school so that I could get a good view of your front door, and I had my sharpshooter just waiting for that guy to show up," Trayvon said. "What guy?" I responded in a perplexed tone with a confused expression on my face. "The guy, the one I know you've been talking to," he said as he looked at me eye-to-eye. I wasn't cheating on him, but I did have male friends from school. He was controlling and didn't like me around any males except for him. "No guys are coming to my house except for you," I replied. "Are you sure? Because Punkin', I'm not having it! I will kill him," he said. Punkin' is the nickname my family has given me. "I'm telling the truth, you have nothing to worry about," I said.

Approximately two weeks later, when he came to visit me, and we were sitting in the living room talking and laughing, as usual. However, he seemed a little preoccupied with his thoughts. We would laugh, and then he would zone out in a blank stare and complete silence.

"What's on your mind?" I asked. He responded, "Nothing, nothing." Then in the same breath, he said, "You know, I love you, right?" "Yes, I do," I responded. "So, I need you to listen to me, okay?" "Okay, what's up?" I said. "Just that if we are out together, and if anyone runs up on me, just run, don't try to stop anyone, just run," he said. "Just run? What's up?" I said. "Don't ask questions; just run." He looked at me seriously—no smile, just seriousness. "Okay," I said and gave him a goodbye kiss as he was about to leave.

Shortly thereafter, the phone rang. My heart fell out of my chest, I dropped the phone, and I screamed to the top of my lungs, "No! No! No! No!" Trayvon had just been killed on Shelton Avenue in front of the Country Market at gunpoint within close-range to his chest. I was told that his chest was so swollen that it exploded on the operating table.

My heart was broken! I cried silently, but I was outwardly angry with the world. Another "man" in my life was gone in an instant!

First, Harvey, my father, and now Trayvon!

Chapter Two

TRAYVON'S DEATH REMINDED ME OF my father, Harvey, who left me when I was eight years old. I loved Harvey with all my heart and everything within me. As a small child, I would watch the hands on the clock closely until the small hand was on the five and the big hand on the half-hour mark. I knew my dad would be walking in the door—smelling like Old Spice cologne and vodka. I would listen for the sound of the doorknob twisting and keys jingling. Just as the door would crack, I knew it was time to go running into daddy's arms.

A Daddy's girl, yep, that was me. He would come home with gifts for his "Punkin' Nickel." I don't know where he got the name, "Punkin' Nickel," but only he called me by that nickname. "Daddy's Home Punkin' Nickel," he would call out, and I would run full force in my Zip Sneakers.

My dad had purchased the zip sneakers from S.S. Kresge's, the department store he worked at in Downtown New Haven, using his employee discount. The Zip Sneaker commercial that would come on the television had every kid in the neighborhood under the mind-set that these sneakers made you run at optimum speed. So, when Daddy called, it was my chance to prove that my Zips worked! I would run to Daddy, jump in his strong arms, and he would swing me around and hold me tight. He would take his rough beard and mustache, and rub it on my face while I tried to dodge his beard tickle, but he would always win. He found it very amusing to see me laugh, duck, and dodge his beard tickle.

"Dad has a gift for you," he said. "You do, Daddy, what is it?" I said as I anxiously awaited him to open the white plastic bag with the word Kresge's written diagonally in blue script, as he stood in the doorway with the front door still open. He didn't have time to close the door behind him because I had bombarded him with my zip run before he could close it. My eyes stayed pierced on the bag, waiting for my gift. Daddy had trained me well, as a little girl, that girls often get gifts.

"I saw this in the store, and I had to get it for you Punkin' Nickel," Daddy said as he pulled out a dark, mustard yellow, short-sleeve t-shirt with a picture of a little girl with messy red hair, freckles, and a big smile with the caption, "I'm the BOSS!"

Oh, yeah, it was right back then I had the characteristics of a boss! I loved the boss t-shirt. I wore the t-shirt every time I got a chance. It had been washed so many times, and it was so worn in spots that you were able to see through it, and holes began to surface.

Daddy was the "ladies" man. Yes, God had blessed him with looks that caught the attention of all of the women—Black, White, Latino, Asian—you name it, and Daddy would capture their attention with his great looks, personality, and humor. He stood about six feet tall, with an even caramel complexion with a hint of red, and a soft evenly picked afro with big curls on the back of his neck, showing that he had Indian blood in his heritage.

Many people would lie and say they were Indian as if they were suffering from an identity crisis and had a problem with being Black. According to family history, Ardelia, Dad's mom, was 100 percent Cherokee Indian, since her mother and father were first cousins to keep the Cherokee bloodline pure.

Dad kept a fresh shave, a thick trim mustache, and sideburns that stopped at his jaw bone in an even straight line. He had small slanted eyes. So, because of his slanted eyes and soft hair, people would think Daddy was mixed Black and Chinese. Daddy definitely was particular about his personal care even when he was in the hospital for his "secret heart attacks," which he would make sure he had a fresh shave. He said, "I can't have these nurses looking at me unshaved." I thought this should be the least of his concerns, but that was my dad. Yes, he had the looks that caught the attention of the women, and he certainly knew it.

God was good to Daddy when God blessed him with looks, but He didn't stop there. God blessed him with the ability to play the organ, piano, write music, and sing! Yes, Dad had the perfect package to be a lady's man. According to Mom, Daddy performing in the night clubs with his band had caused problems in their marriage. In later years, Mom, told me stories of how Dad would be outperforming and would come home intoxicated, smelling like perfume with lipstick on his collar. However, I never saw this side of my daddy. He was perfect in my little girl eyes.

Daddy was a cook. He enjoyed cooking, and I enjoyed eating his food. No one can cook collard greens, black-eyed peas, turkey necks, and potatoes like my daddy cooked them. He could cook anything, and it turned out delicious. He was the master at taking what little we had in the house and making a gourmet meal out of it.

I would stay around in the kitchen while he was cooking because I knew those inviting words would eventually come out of his mouth. "Here Punkin' Nickel, come taste this," Daddy would say. He would look at me, smile, and laugh as I would rub my tummy with a big smile. "Mmmmmm Daddy, this is good, can I have some more?" My favorite place to sit was on Daddy's left leg as he sat on the couch or at the kitchen table. I was always attached to Daddy like a piece of Velcro—I was definitely a Daddy's girl.

Every day of the week, I did the same thing when it was time for him to come home from work. I would look at the clock, wait for the small hand to hit five and the long hand to hit the half-hour mark because I knew shortly after, Daddy would be home, and I would be picked up, swung, around and tickled. I loved my daddy!

Then, suddenly, Daddy didn't come home anymore. I overheard from the family gossip that Daddy had a baby on the way, and it wasn't with my mom. It was painful to lose the man you loved—whether it was your daddy or your first boyfriend.

Chapter Three

REGRETTING THE LOSS OF MY dad was very difficult for me as a small child. I would bury my face in my pillow with my arms across my forehead, and I would cry silently—night after night. My little heart ached and longed for my daddy to come home.

Did I do something wrong? I thought. *Daddy doesn't love me anymore. Wasn't I a good girl?* The thoughts and questions kept coming. Silent tears and deeply hidden hurt, eventually, turned into anger and *resentment* towards my mom. As an adult, *I understand as an adult,* but as a child, *I understood as a child.*

Mom couldn't do anything right—unless she brought Daddy back home. It didn't matter that mom was now a single mother of three children and seven months pregnant while struggling on welfare, getting food stamps, enrolling in college, and ultimately, scared for her life.

I didn't know how to handle my internal hurt and disappointment with Daddy being gone, and I guess, Mom didn't either. I did not express my feelings verbally, but my actions said it all. I wanted to ask Mom for help. But I saw my mother struggling to juggle daily life in this cruel world, and I just didn't want to be another burden.

The words "I love you" came freely from Daddy, but not Mom. I didn't hear the words "I love you" from my mom until I was eighteen and also a mother. As a little girl, I longed to feel loved, but no matter how much I longed for love from my mother, I didn't feel it. She would often remind me, "I'm your mother, not your friend!" I'm not quite sure of her thought process behind her constantly making that statement to me. But...every time I heard those words, they cut deep into my soul. I couldn't understand why my mom couldn't be my best friend; I actually thought she should be. Because of the boundary, she had so vividly set, about not being my friend, I didn't feel comfortable (by any shape or form) when it came to speaking to my mother about any young girl issues. This was especially true when I was molested continuously by my grandmother's boyfriend. I thought she would pick up on my hesitation to go to my Grandmothers, but I guess she read my actions and hesitations as pure disrespect.

My grandmother's boyfriend would constantly tell me, "not to tell anyone because "your mom will be mad at you." Deep down inside, I knew it was wrong, and I silently screamed for help. So, I remained a helpless child with no Daddy at home to protect me. My mother didn't allow us to stay the night at a stranger's houses, so we only went to where she thought was a safe place—Grandma's.

One night, I stayed at Grandma's house, and I was sleeping on the floor. Grandma's boyfriend must have been about to attack me while I was sleep because I woke up to my grandmother saying in a stern, angry voice, "What the heck are you doing over my granddaughter? I will freaking kill you!"

I kept my eyes closed as I pretended to be asleep—like I did every time he forced himself on me. "Oh Berta, you're drunk!" he said. My grandma didn't respond to his reply. I heard her stumbling over the couch. She fell on the white and black leopard fur couch that she had professionally wrapped in plastic to preserve it. I woke up in the morning, and there was Grandma, passed out on the couch, fully dressed with an empty bottle of vodka next to her. I wondered if she was on the couch to guard her grandchild's safety.

My grandma never asked me any questions, and I never spoke a word about the incident. Perhaps, she believed she was too drunk and was hallucinating, or maybe, she didn't remember anything that had happened the night before. As strange as it was, I felt protected for the first time, since the attacks had begun.

Chapter Four

I THANK GOD THAT TODAY, I have a good relationship with my mom. Now, I understand that the chaos was necessary to bring about God's divine order.

As a child growing up, I was very resentful. So, through my eyes at the time, there was nothing that Mom could do right, and through her eyes, I was the child from Hell—the child that couldn't do anything right, the child that gave her the most trouble, and the child destined to fail. So, every month like clockwork, my mother's tolerance for me grew extremely thin. We would end up in a big argument or a physical fight over something as small as leaving a dish in the sink, not moving fast enough when she called, what I had on, how I halfway made my bed, staying in the bathroom too long, or staying in my room too long.

The list of wrongs continued to grow as time went on, and my mom's patience grew thinner. After a while, the complaints about me shifted to "You treat my house like a hotel," and "You're never home." Instead of having a conversation about why I didn't feel at home at our house, I began to feel at home at my best friend's house. Everything was an argument. So, the arguments would often conclude with "Get the hell out of my house!"

By no way was I the best child. I had a mouth that wouldn't stop, and layers of hurt, disappointment, and confusion expressing itself through my temper and anger. I felt out of control, and it was evident when I got into eight physical fights in school in three months and finally, kicked out of school for the third time. Anyone who looked at me sideways was asking to be busted in the face!

Any and everything set me off. I was a ticking emotional time bomb! If during this time, Black families had found it acceptable to seek counseling, instead of thinking a "shrink" was for crazy people, I would have signed myself up. I never even knew that a person existed who could help to put thoughts and emotion in a controllable perspective. All I knew was that I was angry twenty-four hours a day and seven days a week, and I certainly didn't know why. I never questioned how I felt. I just accepted the fact that I was an "angry Black woman". Today, when I hear the phrase, it makes me extremely upset. An angry "Black woman," What does that mean?

In my opinion, Black women have endured more pain, hurt, and rejection from this world, than words in a book would ever be able to express, and unfortunately, many of the deepest scars are from her very own Black man. However, I learned at an early age, being angry was acceptable and considered the norm. So why seek help?

My classmates at Troup Middle School were brutal with their comments and teasing. We were poor. So, I didn't have the latest fashions or an array of clothes to choose from to wear to school. I had three pairs of pants: a washed out black and gray (two-toned pair of pants with raised strips in the front), a pair of classic blue denim, and a pair of sky-blue lightweight jeans, which were about two sizes too big.

I had my favorite sky-blue, lightweight, short sleeve button-up shirt with little white stars on it. This was my favorite shirt because it matched my sky-blue jeans perfectly. I had an off-white knitted V-neck sweater with no sleeves, a long sleeve black t-shirt with a curved neckline, and a few t-shirts that I would put in the rotation. Plus, I had one and a half pairs of shoes. I had a pair with a buckle across the front that at one time was black, later the buckle became blackish and then became grayish due to all of the scuff marks. Then, I had my special color shoes, tan tie-up shoes with little see-through circles all over the shoes and a big hole in the bottom sole, underneath my big toe on the left shoe. I remember putting pieces of a balled-up plastic shopping bag in my shoe to stop my feet from getting wet from the snow. If you're dressed poorly, you are more likely to be judged poorly.

Despite the personal challenges at home and the wardrobe challenges until high school, I was a high honors student and the President of the Beta Club. My teachers were great. I especially became attached to several teachers: Ms. Rosas my Spanish teacher, Mr. Brownell my Science teacher, Ms. Sizemorie my English teacher, and Mr. Sizemorie my Math teacher.

My teachers must have known something was a little different about me because they all took their time with me and showed sincere concern for me. It definitely showed that they loved their profession as teachers because they loved teaching and preparing their students for life. I felt the love from each of these teachers, especially Ms. Rosas. She would give me the hugs that I was missing at home. It was as if God whispered in her ear and told her, "This little girl just needs a hug." So, for these teachers, I performed at my optimum. Some would call me the "teacher's pet," but I wanted to please them and hear them say, "Well done. I'm proud of you."

There was one male, White teacher who taught social studies, who at first, I thought was very kind to me. I was an "A" student in his class. So, on multiple occasions, he wanted to have lunch with me. He would say that I was his favorite student, and he was rewarding me with lunch at Chips, a seafood restaurant in West Haven, CT

I felt this was wrong for a teacher to take me in his car during school hours to have lunch and then sneak me back in the side doors of the school. But I was just being a good girl and listening to my teacher. It came to a sudden stop when we were at Chips, and he asked me to go to his house with him. I must have looked petrified. My eyes began to water, tears flowed down my face, and I dropped my shrimp! I felt so vulnerable as I shook my head from side-to-side to say, absolutely no.

I was frightened. Here I was alone with my teacher, whom I thought was rewarding me, and now he's asking me to come to his home. No one knew I was gone from school, and I had no form of communication to call anyone for help. But this time, I was awake, and I couldn't act like I was asleep. In 2015, I read on Facebook that this same teacher was facing criminal charges for sexual assault with a minor female student. When I read the story, I began to thank God because I believe God stepped in to protect me when I didn't even know it.

A leary teenager becomes a cautious parent.

When it was time for my daughter to go to school, I would always request a female teacher. I'm sure they thought I was being difficult. But they had no idea why I was so adamant, and why I wouldn't bend. I'm sure they had no idea of the story behind the simple request for a female teacher for my precious little girl.

Chapter Five

I'LL NEVER FORGET THE DAY my name was called across the loud-speaker to come to the main office to meet with the Principal, Mr. Beatly. My stomach dropped, and I felt nervous. My mind was racing, and I was trying desperately to recall the last few days. I thought... *Did I do something wrong? Why am I being called to the main office?*

Hesitantly, I was obedient and went to the first floor to the principal's office. I sat on the cold gray metal chair that was next to the main entrance and facing the receptionist. I waited patiently with my hands in my lap, placed together with my fingers interlocking, and fiddling my thumbs because of my nervousness. I couldn't figure out why I was in the principal's office and what in the world was going on. As I sat quietly, I observed all of the commotions in the office.

Students yelling at administrators about their teachers, and teachers were complaining about the student's behavior that was disruptive to the class. After about ten minutes of quietly waiting and watching the people, Mr. Beatly, the principal, came out from the office in the rear on the right side of the general office. Mr. Beatly was always a clean-cut man. His clothes were always neatly in place and never disheveled. He wore a brown suit with even, sharp creases in his pants, a crisp white classic button-up shirt with tan stripes about half an inch apart, and a brown tie with one big diagonal cream color stripe across the middle of the tie. He had an even hazelnut complexion, a short salt and pepper afro, and a thick mustache that reminded me of my dad. He was always upbeat, stood erect, and spoke proper at all times. Mr. Beatly was the only educated Black man in power that I knew.

"Congratulations, Roberta," Mr. Beatly said with a big smile on his face. He continued, "The New Haven Register wants to do a story on a few of our students, and we chose you along with three other students." He must have seen my little slanted eyes stretch big because of my nervousness. "There's nothing to worry about," he said. "A reporter will just shadow you as you carry on your normal school activities. This is a great opportunity for you." He stared at me with a smile awaiting my consent. "Okay," I said as I hung my head. *I guess it wouldn't be a big deal,* I thought to myself. Mr. Beatly handed me a permission slip and said, "Have your parents sign-off on this paperwork and return it to school before the end of the week." After a while, my nervousness turned to happiness. The more I thought about it, the more excited I was.

Wow, the newspaper wants to do an article on me, I thought. However, as soon as the happy thought entered my head, the negative ones showed up. I thought… *I hope they don't take pictures. I'm not cute enough to be in the paper. My hair is a nappy mess.* After overcoming the fear and listening to all of the positive thoughts about being in the newspaper, my mental battle was over, and the positive thoughts won.

I rushed home, excited to tell my mom the good news. "Mom, Mom, Mr. Beatly told me to give you these papers," I said enthusiastically. "What are they about?" she said. "The reporter from the New Haven Register wants to do a story on me and a few other kids in the school on Wednesday." "That's great Punkin, congratulations," my mom said.

My mother smiled and immediately picked up the mustard yellow telephone affixed to the kitchen wall and dialed my grandmother's number. I'm named after my grandmother. She was Roberta Wooten, and I'm proudly Roberta Hoskie, aka 'Little Berta.' Grandma wasn't the typical granny. No, she was far from it. She was a dancer who wore the latest high heels, sipped her vodka, smoked her Newport cigarettes, played her numbers, and cussed like a sailor! She had traveled across the country, back and forth to Canada, as a professional dancer. It was never clear about what she did as a professional dancer, but only what she told me.

She was a flashy dresser—you would see Grandma coming a mile away with her multi-colored sequined jacket and hat. She loved gold, not just dull gold, but flashy liquid gold! She was very much into her appearance. She would never go out of the house without makeup, and there was no convincing her to do otherwise. She was thin and very attractive with a caramel complexion. She would talk to anyone, anywhere, as if she had known them forever. As far as I'm concerned, I had the best grandma ever, and I was fortunate to be her namesake.

I could hear the conversation through the phone as I opened up the brown refrigerator by its broken handle and stared into it as if I were looking for something to eat. I was purposely eavesdropping on the conversation my mom was having with my grandma.

"Hello Gretchen," my grandma said. "Punkin's going to be in the New Haven Register," Mom said in an excited voice. "Get the hell out of here...for what?" Grandma responded as she laughed in joy. "They want to do a story on high-achieving students within the school," Mom added. "Ha, Ha, Ha," Grandma laughed. "Hey, Wilma, Berta is going to be in the paper!" my grandma screamed to her friend, who lived in the same building as she did. "Gretchen, make sure she looks good and don't have her in the paper with a nappy ass head. Do her hair nice," she said. "Oh, Ma," Mom's response was as if she was insulted by the comment. They continued to talk on the phone as my grandmother continued to announce to everyone that she saw in her building that her granddaughter was going to be in the newspaper! I felt happy, and I finally closed the refrigerator and went upstairs to my bedroom.

After Mom hung up the phone, she grabbed her keys to her tan and brown 1980 Vega and said, "I'll be back." Her car was falling apart, but it drove us from point A to point B. We had bicycle wires holding the door closed so that it didn't swing open while mom was driving. Sometimes, when you got into the car, you would have to push up the material that hung down from the inside roof. At one point, it was neatly upholstered, but now, it was falling down in big chunks. However, my mother was grateful for this car because not too long prior to this time, we didn't have a car, and we were catching buses and rides from other people.

Well, when Mom returned, she told me about my appointment with Bob, who had the beauty salon around the corner from where we lived. My brother, Emanuel, worked in his shop sweeping the hair up after haircuts. I was excited because I was about to receive my first perm.

I had always had a lot of hair, and it is thick. There wasn't a lot I could do with it, without a perm, except pull the barrettes to the limit by trying to put my hair in a ponytail. No matter how much I would brush the hair on the back of my neck, it would always pop out and become unmanageable.

So, I was happy to sit in Bob's chair to get my perm. When my Mom returned to pick me up, she was charged an additional fee because I took up two full containers of perm when he normally only used one container. He kept the empty containers as proof to show my mom that he actually had used that much perm treatment on my hair. My mom smiled when she saw me and told me how beautiful I looked. I turned in my seat to look in the mirror, and I smiled from ear-to-ear. I even shook my head from side-to-side just to feel and watch my hair move so easily for the very first time. For the first time in my life, I felt pretty.

Chapter Six

I WAS SO EXCITED BECAUSE tomorrow was the "Big Day!" In preparation, I pulled out my special tan colored shoes from underneath my bed. I ironed my favorite light blue, short sleeve denim shirt, which matched my light blue jeans and my off-white sweater vest. I had spent hours pulling off the little lint balls from the sweater—one-by-one. I didn't have any matching socks, so I gathered a pair of my mother's coffee-colored knee highs, instead. My hair was permed, and Mom had put in the pink hair rollers. I had to look my best just in case they took pictures of me for the newspaper. I took a shower and laid all of my clothes out on the bottom of my bed neatly. I was finally prepared for my big day, and I was definitely going to look my very best! I went to my bedroom window, opened it up, and looked at the dark blue sky with beautiful bright shining stars, and I prayed a special prayer.

> *Dear God, I thank you for today, and I thank you for tomorrow. Bless the people who are less fortunate. Bless the people with no food in Ethiopia, and the kids with the big stomachs on TV. God, help them and help the people who sleep in the streets. And Father, bless me so that I can be a blessing to others. Amen.*

I pulled the handmade quilt up that was on my bed. It had a unique design of multiple patches sewn together with the colors: red, orange, purple, yellow, and off-white. There was no type of sequence to this cover, but it was my favorite. I tapped my little sister on her shoulder and asked her to move over to make room for me. I jumped in the bed, wrapped myself in my favorite quilt, and attempted to go to sleep.

However, I kept counting sheep backward as I looked at the ceiling. I was tired, but going to sleep was a task until I managed to wrap my feet tight with the covers and tuck myself in. Being tightly wrapped in the covers gave me a very calming and secure feeling. I took a deep breath to relax; then I said one more special prayer.

"Father, when I wake up, can You make me pretty? I know You can God. You can do anything. Amen."

Then, I fell fast asleep.

Startled from the loud alarm clock, I jumped out of bed and immediately ran to the mirror anxiously to see if God had answered my prayer overnight. Hoping He had made me pretty with lighter skin without pimples, light eyes, and longer hair—like the little girls on television. I was disappointed again. But this time, I took a deep breath and said, "Well, God, You didn't do it, yet, but I know You can. I'm not upset, God. Because I know, You can do anything."

I showered, got dressed, and Mom did my hair. I was ready for the day. It was a cold, brisk December day. The knee highs and my special tan shoes with the holes on the top and the big hole at the bottom was not a good combination to combat the cold weather during my walk to school. However, I was grateful I had on the white coat that my brother had bought for me. It was the most stylish piece of clothing I owned. It had a diagonal zipper and the extra flap to the slide that I used to cover my mouth with during the wintery walks to school.

My brother, Emanuel, bought this coat for me since he was the oldest, and he understood more than I did about what Mom was going through financially. He understood the situation better than the rest of us. He saw the struggles that Mom was having financially, and he would help out where he could.

I was so happy when he brought home my new coat—the very one that I had seen the advertisement mailer from Kmart. He was genuinely happy for me. Prior to receiving the white coat, I was wearing a black jean jacket that had a torn lining and no pockets. Needless to say, I had many very cold walks to and from school.

Nonetheless, I was so happy and excited when I walked into the school. A classmate approached me as soon as I walked into my homeroom, and he greeted me with, "You finally permed that nappy ass hair!" I was a bit saddened by his mean remarks. It was my very first perm, and I wasn't used to having straight hair. So, I kept moving my bangs out of my eyes so that I could see the chalkboard. My mom had curled my bangs, but after a while, the curls kept falling in my face. "I didn't know you had good hair," another girl said. I didn't respond to either classmate; I just pulled my books out of my book bag and focused on the teacher.

At 8:15 a.m., a woman, with shoulder-length, dusty blonde hair walked in wearing a red three-quarter length puff coat with a knitted matching scarf and mittens. I knew she was the reporter since she had video equipment in her hands. "Hello, I'm Kim from the New Haven Register, and I'm looking for Roberta Hoskie," she said. The teacher pointed to me, and I raised my hand, so she was able to identify me. The reporter had a very calming spirit and a nice smile. She sat right behind me. "Hello, Roberta. My name is Kim, and I'm the reporter for the Register," she said as she extended her hand out for me to shake. "Hello," I said and smiled. "Continue to go about your day, as usual. I will be silent, and you won't even notice that I'm here," she said with a big smile.

Shortly after Kim's greeting, the school bell rang, indicating it was time to change classes. The halls quickly filled with over 500 students hurriedly rushing to get to class on time. It was pretty obvious to everyone that I was being followed. At the time, Troup Middle School consisted predominantly of African American students, and Kim was a tall, White woman, who stood out to the students like a sore toe and thumb. They knew she wasn't a teacher because a teacher wouldn't be following me around with a tape recorder.

The students were watching her every move. I was extremely nervous, and my heart began beating fast while taking deep breaths and counting silently to three before I let it out. I thought to myself... *One more thing to give my classmates to tease me about.*

I clearly heard the half-suppressed laughter mixed with whispers, "Who is she?" I held my head down to avoid eye contact with the students, especially Dre, the boy who had stayed back a grade that I had a secret crush on. He was popular, and all of the girls thought he was so handsome. I would daydream about having a conversation with Dre—almost every day. I would practice talking to him in the mirror at home, but I never had enough courage to say a single word to him. Instead, I avoided him like the plague. Dre never looked my way. I was a quiet good girl, and Dre liked big mouth, bad girls. I was sure that he didn't even know I existed.

The day was unusually uncomfortable; however, it went by fast. Having someone take pictures of everything you do, including writing notes to your friends in class was a bit awkward, to say the least. But not as awkward as it was to have lunch with a complete stranger who was acting like they are not there.

Later in the day, Kim said, "Before I leave, I would like to get a picture of everyone on the steps of the school." "Okay," we answered in unison. When we walked outside to take the picture, it was freezing cold. You could see the steam coming from our mouths when we talked. "This will be fast," the photographer said. "Let's get the two boys on the outside and the two girls in the middle. Girls put your hands together, pull them to your face, and let your chin rest in your hands," the photographer said. I tried to hold the pose, but by my bangs kept falling in my face. So, after about five takes, we heard, "Great job, we are all finished for today!" I was certainly relieved when I heard those words, "all finished".

The next morning, I woke happy and was feeling special because of the previous day's activities. I got ready for school, as usual, and I wore my washed black two-toned jeans, a t-shirt, and my special tan shoes. It was an awesome morning!

On my way to School, I noticed, The New Haven Register was on the doorsteps of the entire neighborhood, and I was on the Front Cover! I felt like a celebrity! I felt SPECIAL, and it felt GOOD! "Wow, That's me on the cover of the newspapers. Thank you, God," I said. I smiled for the entire walk to school as I looked at all of the newspapers on the porches. I was on top of the world. This was one of the happiest days of my Life.

As soon as I opened the school door, Dre, my imaginary boy-friend, was running up the stairs toward me. I immediately put my head down. *No eye contact,* I thought. Just then, my day got better, and my dream came true! "Roberta," Dre said. I looked up in surprise, thinking that this was the moment I was waiting for with my inno-cence. The moment we finally have a real conversation; the moment he notices me. "Yes," I responded. "I saw you in the Register," he over excitedly said. Then, he pulled out the paper from his back pocket, open it, and said very loudly with a loud laugh, "And you had a big freaking hole in your shoe!"

He laughed so loud and boisterous that he demanded the atten-tion of the other students in the hall. He repeated, "Look at the big hole in her shoe!" as he held up the front page of the New Haven Register so that everyone in the stairwell could see. Then, he pointed to my special tan shoes and said, "Look, she has them on, now!" He laughed so loud and so hard that I was humiliated.

I ran up the stairs as fast as I could while holding back my tears. I quickly ran to the bathroom, opened the first stall, put the seat down, and closed the door so that no one could see me. I began crying. I wanted to go home and bury my face in my pillow. I cried so long that I missed homeroom class as I sat in the bathroom stall crying my heart out.

I cried so hard that I began hyperventilating. Until that point in my life, I had thought holes in shoes were normal. I looked down at my shoes, twisted my ankle to the outside, and just stared at it—the big hole in my shoe. Tears flowed uncontrollably. I just watched my tears drop on the bathroom floor, one-by-one while I grew numb to what just had happened. My shoe hole was on the front page of the New Haven Register, and there was no hiding it. It was on everyone's porch waiting to be viewed.

To this day, I keep the picture to remind me of just how far I've come from poverty!

Chapter Seven

I WENT FROM BEING THE quiet good girl with high honors to the bad girl gone wrong. I was expelled from multiple schools because I was fighting on an average of twice a week. As a result, fighting became my new normal. Word spread in the streets fast. My male cousins would call me when any female made them upset. After a while, all my cousins had to say was, "I'm calling my cousin Punkin'". The girls knew what that meant, and those words alone were a strong enough warning for the female to leave them alone or to start acting right. Word had spread everywhere.

"Did you whip her butt?" my grandmother asked me as she stood over the sink watching the water run to do dishes while she smoked her Newport cigarette and drank her vodka. "I know you, Berta, you whipped that girl's butt, Huh, you are my namesake and Grandma don't take no stuff. That girl didn't know what the heck was going on when you busted her upside the head with that lock. I bet that chick will think twice before she messes with you again! Huh?" My grandma took another puff of her cigarette. "Well, she knows now!" I replied. "Ha, you ain't nothing to play with, Berta. And your mother called me all upset because you had the police at her house. They said you chased a girl down and beat her with a baseball bat and put the girl in the hospital? Berta, you surely got my temper, but you can't be beating people up with bats unless they're too big. Then, you find anything and knock their freakin' head off!"

Grandma took another puff from her cigarette, put her glass under the running water, swirled the water around, and took a sip. "But, Grandma," I replied, "I didn't start this one. I didn't even know her. I was getting off the bus on Dixwell and cutting through the parking lot behind the Stetson Library, and three ugly, gorilla-looking girls came up to me. She said, 'Are you messin' with my man?' I ain't messing with her man. I didn't even know the boy's name that she said. I told her, I didn't even know the guy. Then she tells me that I'm lying. I said, I ain't lying. Why I gotta lie to you? You ain't nobody. Then, before I knew it, all three of them started swinging on me and jumped me in the parking lot. So, I told her that it wasn't over. I don't know if she thought I was just playin'. But, I called my girls and found her right on Goffee Street." "Goffee Street? She lives in the same apartments you do?" "No. I think her cousin lives in the house by the barbershop. She didn't give me a fair one, so she doesn't get a fair one! When I saw her, I went 'black,' and I took that bat and chased her up the street, beatin' her with the bat until she passed out!" "Well, I'm glad she didn't die" "Me, too," I said, as I cringed at the thought.

"Hope you don't get in too much trouble with the law, you don't need no criminal record. You gonna be an attorney, so you're gonna have to ignore these girls and figure out how you can get back into school. I know you got your temper honestly but be better than Grandma. You gonna be a rich attorney, Berta, your education is important. You know, I only went to school until the third grade, I had to work for them white folks, then my mama got sick, and I had to take care of my brothers and sisters. I had your mom when I was only fourteen, but I ain't know nothin' about sex, all I knew is I liked your grandad. I didn't know what he was doing, and then a month later, I'm pregnant. My mother never talked to me about boys or nothin'. I did the best with what I had. Your mom never went hungry even if we ate grits for dinner; she wasn't hungry. Your grandfather went away in the Vietnam war and came back a different man. He wasn't the 'Jeff' I knew. When he came back, he was a violent, angry, and he started beatin' on me. So, I had to leave him," Grandma explained as she took a puff of her cigarette and another swig of her drink.

"Oh, Grandma, I didn't know that," I said. "Yes, Berta, Grandma done been through a lot, but you got to be better. I pushed your mom to get her education, and now, my daughter has a master's degree in Psychology," Grandma said with such a sense of pride as if my mother completing college was her greatest accomplishment.

My grandmother stared at the water that was still running in the kitchen sink. For a moment, she went into deep thought and made an expression as if she had an epiphany. She puffed on a cigarette and began a serious conversation with me about generational curses with the women in our family and how I had to be better than them. "My mom had me at twelve, I had your mom at fourteen, and your mom had your brother at eighteen. We were all young and had to struggle. Don't let no boy pop you up; it's going to mess up everything, and you won't be that rich attorney. You will have to get on the State (welfare), and things will be hard. This world ain't fair," she took another puff of her cigarette and continued talking.

"This fighting, you are doing, Berta, I laugh and joke, but it ain't good. Women in our family have hot heads, and it does not end up good. Your Aunt Fannie, she would fight men and women up and down Congress Avenue, back in the day. One time, she came out fighting with two big 'ole butcher knives—One knife in one hand, and one knife in the other hand. Fannie went to fighting, and blood was everywhere!" Grandma took another puff of her cigarette and a sip of her vodka as she went down memory lane with me.

"Fannie ended up doing time," she paused again as if going down a painful memory lane. "Your Aunt Mammie, my baby sister, wasn't a fighter. She took a lot, but when she was up against the wall, you better watch out! Her boyfriend used to beat on her badly. One day, he beat her really bad and then wanted her to have sex with him. Mammie went on and slept with him, but afterward, while he was sleeping, she went into the kitchen, pulled out the big black pot, went to boiling water, and made some grits. When the grits were done, she called the police. Then she went right in that room where he was sleeping and poured the grits all over his naked body. It gave him third-degree burns. She knew what she was doing when she called the police, and she timed it perfectly. Then, can you believe it? Those two got back together after the grits episode. You would have thought that he learned his lesson, but he was a crazy fool. He was a black belt in Karate, his hands were a licensed weapon, and he still was beating on her. He beat her so bad one day that her eye was about as big as my fist, black and blue. One time, he went to beat on her, and she was ready. I don't know who gave it to her, but she had a gun, and she shot him, paralyzing him for life. She ended up in jail," she took another puff of her cigarette and continued after another thoughtful moment.

"Now, your Aunt Gloria, she was a fighter. I remember one time, she beat up my old boyfriend, Ronnie. I mean a fist fight and she beat him down. Your mother said that she never saw a female fight like your Aunt Gloria. Gloria did some time in jail, too."

My grandmother's stories of her sisters really made me think. It wasn't just a coincidence that they were fighters, maybe it was something in the bloodline. Maybe, it really was a generational curse trying to raise within me. I had just finished beating a girl unconscious with a baseball bat. *What if she would have died?* I thought. Then history would have repeated itself, and I would be in jail doing time.

I loved my grandma. I could talk to her about anything, and she would tell me the truth. She gave me her old school wisdom. I looked around her small, 5'x3' kitchen and was saddened that she didn't live where she wanted to live. She would talk about owning a home someday, but the cost was too expensive. She said that when she hits the numbers, she would buy her a house quick, fast, and in a hurry. Winning the lottery or the numbers, as the older folks called it, was and still is the dream of most people who have lived in poverty.

"Grandma, when I become a rich attorney, I'm going to buy you your own house with a backyard where you can plant your tomatoes and collard greens," I said in a daze, daydreaming how it would feel to give my grandmother something that she was never able to obtain for herself.

During this era, owning a home was still the American Dream. Grandma had lived in a 400 square foot efficiency apartment for years. Her apartment was cluttered. When you walked into her apartment, you would have to turn sideways to get through the kitchen. You would have to squeeze between the makeshift stool and the big deep freezer that she kept filled with meat from Ferraro's meat market. She said that she always kept the deep freezer filled with food, just in case, my mom ran out of food for us.

Glass knick-knacks, old magazines, clothes, and shoes cluttered her apartment, but she still managed to keep her apartment immaculate. I pulled out a real estate magazine from my oversized, black, over the chest pocketbook. I picked up the real estate magazine from C-Town market on my way to her house. I flipped through the pages and found a two-family flat home in Hamden, just over the New Haven town line. "Look at this house, Grandma, this is nice for you. It's brick with everything on one level, and there is another house attached to it where I can live. I'm going to get you this home, Grandma," I said with pride. My grandmother smiled and said, "Good Berta, I would love that."

Chapter Eight

"YOU WON'T DISRESPECT ME AGAIN! Get the *Hell* out of my house! You're too much trouble!" My mother said as she swung her fist towards my head. I put my hands up, stopping her from hitting me and pushed her back.

"I brought you in this world, and I'll take you out of here!" My mother's voice escalated as she was extremely upset. She continued, "You make your bed hard, and you lay in it! You don't respect me or my house, so get out!" My mom went to swing to hit me again, I stopped her, and our arms were locked together since I was not allowing her to hit me anymore. "I'll get out your house! I don't want to be here, anyway! Some type of mother you are!" I screamed at the top of my lungs. "You don't want to live here. Get out, go find your good-for-nothing father. He ain't did nothing for you a day in your life," she yelled. "I will find my dad," I responded. "Good luck, He's good-for-nothing, absolutely, nothing and he has nothing! I took care of you; not him!"

With tears streaming down my face as I huffed and puffed with so much anger; you would have thought that I was fighting a stranger on the street. "You didn't take care of me because you let me be sexually abused! I was screaming for help when you were downstairs, and you didn't come!"

It had finally come out after over six years of acting like everything was okay. I finally told her in the midst of one of the biggest fights we had ever had. My mother's eyes got big, and her entire mood shifted. "What?" she shockingly asked. "You didn't protect me! You were right downstairs; he took me in your room, he told me you knew what he was doing, and you sent him upstairs." I screamed with tears flowing, both of my fists balled-up as tight as possible, and my arms board straight on the side of me. She looked at me with glassed eyes and innocence. She said in an utterly heartbroken tone, "I didn't know that, I never knew such a thing."

The house got quiet, my mom, asked more detailed questions about the encounters, and she finally said that she would talk to me later about it. I felt so relieved. After all of these years of carrying this heavy burden and not telling anyone about what was happening to me; I finally felt a burden lifted. I wasn't happy that it came out in the heat of an argument, but I was glad that the gigantic secret burden of all of the hurt had finally come out in the open. I believed my mom when she said that she didn't know anything about it. I wish I would have told her sooner since there was such a sense of relief that I didn't even know I longed for. I had so many mixed emotions—from tears of anger to tears of relief, and finally, to tears of joy. The joy came in knowing that my mom wasn't involved in this heinous abuse.

As I think back, it's really amazing how a young person's thought process can be so easily manipulated—especially, young girls with low self-esteem. But that's what abusers do—they lie to keep control of the victim.

A few days went by before my mom brought up the abuse situation. I wondered, if my mother would fight him, or call my dad to tell him to go and beat my abuser down. Would my grandmother put him out? I wondered what good would come out of me finally telling my secret to my mom. I even thought about how I would testify in court—I would just tell the truth about everything.

I wasn't scared of him anymore. He deserved to rot underneath the jail cell for what he did to me, and I'm sure, I wasn't his first victim. Then, I thought that it would boil down to my word against his word; surely, he would deny it, and the judicial system might even believe him over me. Besides, he was an old White man, and I was just another young, Black girl.

"Let's talk for a moment," my mother said to me as we were upstairs in the hallway. She paused as if to get her thoughts together. "Punkin', I was thinking, and it's best if we just don't say anything to anyone. Grandma doesn't need to know. So, let's just keep this to ourselves," she said. "Okay," I replied, and I walked to my room. I laid on my bed with my face in my pillow, and I burst into a hysterical silent cry. I punched the mattress as hard as I could and stuffed the pillow into my mouth to mute my screaming. The gigantic secret burden that I thought was finally out in the open was just shoved back in from the only person that I thought could and would actually help me.

Needless to say, the fighting between us ultimately started back up. However, this time, she dropped me off at the Douglas House, a teenage shelter on Howard Avenue in New Haven, and told the representatives, "I don't want her anymore, and you can have her." She said it like she was dropping off a pet at a shelter, instead of her daughter, whom she had loved, cared about, and had raised from birth.

Chapter Nine

"YOU CAN HAVE HER," WERE the last words my mom said while looking at me as if I was the scum of the earth. She turned her lip up, rolled her eyes, walked away, and didn't look back. I stood in the doorway in complete silence.

I was fourteen years old—the age when a daughter needs her mother the most, and she had given up on me. I had been through emotional turmoil almost my entire life, and when I finally shared with her about the years of abuse, she turned her back on me. I had hoped my mom could understand that my acting out was me screaming for help, but instead, I ended up in a homeless shelter. Did she even consider my hopeless state—I was a girl, only fourteen, and what could happen to me in the homeless shelter? Or…did it even matter to her at this point?

The shelter was in many ways like a juvenile prison. When you walked in the front door, there was a dim lit hallway with worn beige 12x12 tiles that lead to the registration desk, which was enclosed with what appeared to be bulletproof plastic. It had a small sliding window, big enough to pass the clipboard through to sign in and to sign out. After signing in, I would get buzzed into the 12'x14' main area, where we were allowed to congregate and watch the one television in the entire facility. To the left of that area was a 12'x9' meeting room, which the staff used for their meetings. The room would also serve as the visitor area.

We weren't allowed to have any visitors unless they were on the visitor's list—very much like a prison. All of the activities were very structured. There was a chalkboard hanging on the wall next to the staircase just before we entered the kitchen area. On the chalkboard was a list of chores to be completed by the residents. It included the resident's name and the time the chore must be completed. Everyone within the shelter was assigned various tasks throughout the entire house.

I used to be upset when I had the kitchen duty, which meant that I had to wash all of the dishes after dinner from every person that lived in the shelter, including the pots and pans that were used to prepare the dinner. However, I would gladly accept the kitchen duties over having to clean and scrub the filthy bathroom. The bathroom smelled like old urine with old bloody maxi pads on the floor and the side of the trash can. It was completely unsanitary. Urine was all over the seats and the floor. I plugged my nose every time I had to go to the bathroom, so cleaning it was definitely a chore (pun intended).

Bedtime was at 8 p.m. sharp! There was a bell that rang to notify residents when it was time to go upstairs to go to bed. We slept in a room with several bunk beds lined up against the wall, and if you were lucky, you would get to sleep on one of the single beds. The beds were made of dark metal wiring braided together with a very thin mattress on top. We were able to feel the metal through the mattress, which made it very hard to sleep.

Just as there was a bell to signal that it was time to go to sleep, there was another bell to wake everyone up to get ready for school. Getting a ride to and from school by the shelter employees was embarrassing. I would ask to be dropped off and picked up on the backside of the school, so the other students didn't see me getting out of the shelter van.

There was such heartbreaking loneliness in the shelter, and there wasn't any love around, either. I was so hurt because I was in a shelter and no one cared. I had a family, but where were they? I thought over and over... *Where are the people who care about me?* And I couldn't find anyone. I didn't know if my other family members actually knew that I was in the shelter. I was too afraid to ask for fear of what they might say. I didn't want to know that they knew and realize they had done nothing to help me. I was too afraid of reaching out for help and then getting rejected. My heart was broken.

I had my dad's phone number on a ripped piece of paper that I had carried around for years. The paper was worn, but I kept it with me in case of an emergency. The phone number was in a different area code (912), so calling from Connecticut meant it would be a long-distance cost, but this was an emergency, he needed to know that his "Punkin' Nickle" had no one, and she needed him.

So, I managed to sneak in the administration office while they were having a meeting to call him. I was planning my escape call to my dad for days. I knew the office routine, so when they went into their Saturday morning staff meeting at 9 a.m., I crawled into the office and pulled out my wrinkled piece of paper with my dad's phone number on it.

My heart was pounding because I didn't want to get caught. I didn't want to get kicked out because then, I would be living on the street. At least, I had food and a bed here. But... I had to talk to my dad. He had to know what was going on. He would surely, get on the next train and take his "Punkin' Nickle" with him. He wouldn't have me living in a homeless shelter. I just had to contact him. So, the risk of breaking into the administration office was worth it for me. I had already played out the conversation in my head. *"Dad, it's me. I'm in a homeless shelter, and I need you to come to get me,"* I would say. In my plans, my dad would be surprised, ask me for the address, and the next day, he would show up at the door to take me with him.

This was the moment I had planned for and waited for—patiently. With my heart pounding, and my palms sweating from my nervousness, I picked up the phone and began to dial my dad's number. Ring, ring, ring, and on the third ring, I heard someone coming near the office. I quickly hung the phone up and hide under the desk in a fetal position, holding my breath, being completely still, and as quiet as possible. My heart was pounding hard, and I could hear it pumping from within my body. It was loud to me, and I was afraid that the staff person could hear my pounding heart because it was the one thing I couldn't control.

I watched a pair of scuffed up, worn white new balance sneakers with a navy blue "N" symbol on the side of it, walk by the desk. He grabbed papers from the copier, and then he left. I waited a few minutes to make sure I didn't hear anyone else, then I came out from underneath the desk and began to dial again.

Ring, ring, ring, ring, ring. It seemed like the phone rang endlessly. Finally, I heard the phone connects and anxiously, I blurted out, "Dad, it's me, I'm in..." But before I could finish my sentence, I heard the operator say, "The number you have reached is not in service; please hang up and dial again. This is a recording."

I hung my head, paused, closed my eyes, and said, "God, WHY?" I slammed the phone down. My last bit of hope was gone. I had no contact with any family member who would be willing to take me in to live with them. I walked out of the administration office with no fear, just disappointed with life. At this point, the thought of being caught didn't even cross my mind.

Depression began to sink in. I sat down in the chair by the window. I went into a deep daze as I stared through the iron bars on the window looking at the people directly across the street; they were having a family cookout. The music was playing loudly. People were dancing and having a good time—having family fun. A card game was going on, and the girls were playing Double Dutch and Hopscotch. The boys were riding their bicycles up and down the block. Hot dogs and hamburgers cooked on the little red grill. I wanted to be there so badly. I wanted to play Double Dutch, too. I was hungry. I wanted to eat. I wanted a hamburger cooked on the grill, on a lightly grilled bun with ketchup. The food smelled so good as I continued to watch the family across the street enjoy their sunny, Saturday, family cookout.

Then, the emotional volcano erupted, and big teardrops began to fall down my face as I realized the house that I was staring at through the bars was my Aunt's home. It was my family, who were eating, playing Double Dutch, and having a good time—without me. Feeling abandoned was an understatement.

Looking back on the bad times, none of the staff left a favorable impression on my life. In fact, I cannot even recall the name of any of the staff. And that alone speaks volumes to the lack of love or even humanity in the atmosphere of the shelter—truly homeless.

This also speaks as a lesson learned: you should never look down on people going through hard times because you have no idea where God is bringing them to. I'm sure the staff thought that I was just another "Black girl gone bad." They had no idea of the future before me, or that what I was going through was going to build a stronger testimony to put in this book you're reading right now.

Chapter Ten

I WAS AT MY ALL-TIME low. Depression was slowly taking over. My thoughts of being unloved began to plague me. I wasn't eating because I had lost my appetite. I didn't speak to anyone. I would do my chores, stare out the window, and wouldn't utter a single word to anyone. Not even Wanda, one of my roommates, who had a bubbly personality. She could spark a conversation with anyone, anywhere, at any time. Somehow, I couldn't fix my mouth to say what I was thinking. Because I knew if I did, I would have a mental breakdown. I had no life coping skills—none for this hard life—at such an early age.

This certainly wasn't the life portrayed on "The Cosby Show," my favorite television show at the time. The Cosby's were so happy—the idealistic Black family unit. The father was a doctor, the mother was an attorney, the children were all well-loved, and they lived in a beautiful home. This show was how I desired my life to be like. But instead, my reality was more like "The Punky Brewster Show". Our similarities were comparable: her name was Punky, and my name was Punkin', she was abandoned by her parents, and so was I.

"Roberta, you have a visitor, I heard over the intercom system." Who would be visiting me? Since I thought that no one cared. Every day in the shelter was the same thing and the same structure. The only time there was a deviation in the daily plan was if someone had a visitor, and that didn't happen often. The only somewhat of consistency of visitation that I had was when my godparents and my god-sister, Nikki visited. They would sometimes come by after church, every other Sunday and spend time with me in the visitor's room.

Nikki was one of my best friends, and her parents, Robert and Cynthia Pulley, were pastors at the Outreach for Christ Lifeline Ministries. They had become my godparents by default. Nikki's family was the only family, I knew of, that had both a Mother and a Dad present in the home.

I admired my godmother on multiple levels. She was funny, energetic, compassionate, and for some reason, she had a unique way of making me feel loved. Mama Cynthia always dressed her best. She had the best shoes, all different colors: blue shoes, red shoes, silver shoes, gold shoes, clear shoes; you name it, and she had them. She also had the most flashest outfits to match!

Dad Pulley was sharp in his suits as well. They made such a nice-looking couple. Dad Pulley was a "no-nonsense, holiness preacher," who took on the Five-Fold ministry. He was a pastor, teacher, evangelist, apostle, and certainly a prophet.

I was given multiple prophecies from my godfather, godmother, and others. It's important that I take the time to show theses prophecies and how they have been fulfilled because you may have prophecies that you may have given up on. This section is to inspire you NOT to give up on your prophecies. You must trust God and wait on them to happen.

LIST OF SOME OF MY PROPHECIES AND OUTCOMES

1) **Prophecy**—I will be wealthy, and I will own multiple companies.
   a) *Prophecy fulfilled*
      i) 2004, Opened Outreach Property Management
      ii) 2011, Opened Outreach Realty Services
      iii) 2011, Opened Outreach School of Real Estate
   b) *Age when the prophecy was given*
      i) Age fourteen through twenty-eight.
   c) *Given By*
      i) Bob Pulley, Cynthia Pully, and Countless Others

54

2) **Prophecy**—I would be on the cover of newspapers.
   a) *Prophecy fulfilled*
      i) 2015, I was on the cover of New Haven Register as the "Person of the Year".
      ii) 2017, I was on the cover of newspapers around the world, including the country of Cyprus.
   b) *Age when the prophecy was given*
      i) Sixteen
   c) *Given by*
      i) Bob Pulley

3) **Prophecy**—I would live in a house bigger and better than any house I had seen at the time.
   a) *Prophecy fulfilled*
      i) 2016, I moved into a house with a value that is close to a million dollars.
   b) *Age when the prophecy was given*
      i) Fourteen to sixteen—off and on until my late twenties.
   c) *Given by*
      i) Bob Pulley, Cynthia Pulley, and multiple others

4) **Prophecy**—My name will be known across the world.
   a) *Prophecy fulfilled*
      i) 2017, I was on international news, and the story went viral on social media, hitting over thirty-five million views worldwide.
      ii) 2018, I spoke before 20,000 people from twenty-six different countries.
   b) *Age when the prophecy was given*
      i) Fourteen through Sixteen
   c) *Given by*
      i) Bob Pulley and Cynthia Pulley

5) **Prophecy**—There are women, whom God has called you to lead.
   a) *Prophecy fulfilled*
      i) 2016, I founded the Millionaire Mindset Sisterhood, a faith-based sisterhood, devoted to "breaking the poverty curse".
   b) *When the prophecy was given*
      i) Early 2000s, 2104, and 2015
   c) *Given by*
      i) Cynthia Pulley and Kelontae Gavin

6) **Prophecy**—I would write a book that would help many people across the world, and I wouldn't be able to count them.
   a) *Prophecy fulfilled*
      i) 2019, I Published my first book, *The Poverty Curse Broken: The Roberta Hoskie Story. (The book you're reading right now.)*
   b) *Age when the prophecy was given*
      i) Teenager
   c) *Given by*
      i) Bob Pulley

If God has said it, believe it, and wait on it. If you're waiting on prophecies to be fulfilled, know that God's timing is not, our timing. We tend to want things *right now*. We live in a world of immediate gratification, and God doesn't. The above list could go on and on, but I chose only to highlight a few to encourage you, to show that in today's day and age, prophecy is still real, and it will come to pass.

Now back to the Story…

I was happy to hear that I had visitors. It was Sunday, around 3 p.m., so I knew it was the Pulleys coming to check on me and to give me encouraging words. They were the only people whom I would allow to break my silence. At the time, I didn't know why they took a special liking for me, but today, I know that it was all in God's plan.

I went into the visitor's room, and there they were smiling and looking at me as if this was a happy day. I was depressed, but the depression spirit didn't stand a chance around them. Their happy energy was contagious, so in their presence, I was happy.

Nikki caught me up on the latest gossip with her boyfriend, Todd. My godparents gave me an abbreviated version of the Sunday message that my godfather had delivered earlier in the day. They stayed for an hour, the maximum time for visitation. There was a light knock on the door, "Five minutes until visitation is over," the Staff employee said, as she peeked her head through the cracked door.

They visited me in the shelter on multiple occasions, and each time before they would leave, my godfather would say, "Let's have a word of prayer." This particular prayer gave me chills from the top of my head to the sole of my feet.

Father Lord, in the Name of Jesus, we ask that You bless Punkin' and that Your spirit dwells within her. Father, we thank You because Lord, even in this, You are at work. Help Punkin' to see that the chaos in her life is only to bring about Your Divine order for her life. Help her to realize, God, that although, she is in a shelter that You are her true shelter and that You will never leave her or forsake her. Father, I know You have set her aside for Your Glory. I know Your Perfect Will, will be done in her even when she doesn't understand. Father anoint her for Your Will, for I know, without a shadow of a doubt, that her life has a purpose for You and Your Kingdom, in Jesus name I pray.

And we all said, *"AMEN" together.*

The employees must have wanted some of that good prayer. They stood on the other side of the door listening. I saw their shadows. I pointed at them to Nikki, and she just shook her head.

"Punkin', It doesn't matter, what it looks like, you're destined for greatness," my godmother said in a stern voice, looking at me eye-to-eye.

"I promise you, daughter, God spoke to me and told me that He has a great plan for your life, and that you will lead millions all over this world and that God will get the glory! You won't have to want for anything. God's Spirit of Wealth will dwell all on you, my daughter. God told me that He has a plan and to trust Him to turn everything around for your good." Tears began to run down my godmother's face as she felt God's spirit when she spoke.

"Don't focus on who hurt you, or who did you wrong. Look past your problems and focus on the Problem Solver. This, my daughter, is the key to keeping your sanity. What the Devil is trying to use to take you out, mark my words, God will use it for His good!"

My godmother hugged me and said, "Now, go get your stuff; you're coming home with us."

Chapter Eleven

THE SHIFT

"THAT'S RIGHT, PUNK, YOU'RE COMING home with us!" Nikki said with a big smile showing her braces. Nikki would call me Punk, short for Punkin'. "For real?" I replied as I looked at my godparents. They both smiled at me, nodded their heads, and said, "For Real." I hugged Nikki, my godparents, and joined in on the group hug. It was so emotional, and no one had a dry eye. I ran upstairs and grabbed my bag of belongings from the corner of the room next to my bunk bed as my godparents spoke to the representative of the homeless shelter. I was so happy, and I moved as fast as I could. I was about to be free, and I was going to stay with people who loved me and make me feel like family—yes, a real family. I was their daughter, and no one could tell me different.

The black Astro van with a thick gold stripe along the bottom was parked outside. The door slid open; then I took one more look at the shelter as I was getting in the van. I saw Wanda in the window, one of the girls that I had befriended while staying in the Douglas House. She stared out the window, watching me leave. I stared back, waved goodbye slowly and got into the car.

I was happy to be on my way to my new home with my godparents, but I felt bad for Wanda. Her mother was a crackhead, and she had never met her father. She had been abused—physically and mentally. I knew then that she didn't have much hope for her future. She almost got kicked out of the shelter on numerous occasions because of her jumping out of the window to meet up with multiple boys after midnight. I said a quick prayer for her, but even as a child, my spirit was grieved. I couldn't explain it, but I just knew life was going to be hard for her.

Several years later, I saw her on the news charged with sexual assault and kidnapping. She ended up being strung out on PCP, committing a litany of crimes, and finally ended up doing time in and out of jail.

Prior to living with my godparents, I had never seen the inside of a single-family home. All of my family members either lived in the projects or lived in an apartment near the projects. I was amazed at how open the house felt. My godmother studied my reactions and took her time walking me through each room of the house, letting me slowly take it all in.

She opened up the slider doors to the backyard and said, "We get deer back here all the time. They just sit down, and they don't bother anyone." "Deer? That's scary," I said. "No, it's not. It's peaceful, and they don't bother anyone." Just as she was explaining, a deer began to walk into the backyard. "Look, Punkin', there's a deer right in between those bushes," she said as she pointed to the deer. I looked up, and I saw a deer up close and personal for the first time in my life. Deer just don't come in the hood. We had alley cats, stray dogs, and raccoons with rabies walking around during the day, but no deer.

She continued on the tour of the house. I was even more amazed when I walked into the master bedroom. My mouth opened in surprise to see a bathroom in her bedroom! "Oh, my goodness, you have a bathroom in your bedroom!" I said in a surprised, excited tone. I walked in the bathroom, pulled the shower curtains back, and yes, there was a shower, too! It was just amazing and such an eye-opener.

God knew that this moment was necessary for me. I had to be exposed to greater things in life. He had to show me that there is much more in life than the environment I was in, and God had to show me prosperity through people who looked like me. I'm sure that if it was a White man or a White woman, the effects wouldn't have been the same. My thoughts would have immediately canceled out the fact that I could live like this. I would have told myself, "They are White, and this is how White people live." But God didn't give me that excuse.

My godfather was from Brooklyn, and my godmother was from the projects in New Bern, NC. So, God said, "No Excuses." "You will have a house like this Punkin', and you will have an even better house than this," she said. I stopped, looked around, paused, and replied, "I can, how?" with a serious look on my face. "What do you want to be when you grow up?" "I want to be an attorney," I said. "Great, Punkin', you can be an attorney. I believe in you. The key to success is to keep putting God first. He will give you the desires of your heart; never ever doubt Him, and He will deliver," she responded. "When I finally make it out of the hood, I ain't never going back!" I said, and I imagined living in a suburban area for the first time in my life. I took a deep breath closed my eyes, and just imagined how life could be in my future. My imagination was vivid, and it felt so real that it startled me. "Remember, you can be anything you want to be, Punkin'. You can be an attorney, a doctor, a business owner, or anything. You don't have to be a product of your environment. Just trust God and promise me that you'll remember this." "I will, Ma, I promise," I said. "Good. Now, let's go watch my favorite movie, 'Pretty Woman.'"

My godmother and I went into her den and simply watched a movie. It was such a good bonding experience. I will never forget how much she enjoyed the movie. She laughed so much when Julia Roberts went shopping on Rodeo Drive, especially, after the women looked down on Julia for not being as "professionally polished" as they were. "Rodeo Drive, baby! Whew Punkin', that's the place to shop girl. Yes, Rodeo Drive," my godmother said as she cheered for Julia Roberts as the *underdog*.

The Pulley's took me in as their own child as if they didn't already have a large family to take care of—besides Nikki, they had four sons and one daughter, totaling six children—and seven, if you counted me. I had to know, so I asked my godmother, "Why did you come and get me?" She explained, "When we would leave from visiting you, my spirit was uncomfortable. I knew that behind the hard shell was a young girl crying for help. God spoke to my heart, and He told me to bring you home with us and to treat you like one of our own. He showed me that you are 'destined for greatness' in your life." "Destined for greatness." Well, that was a phrase that I would hear countless times over the next few years.

The feeling, I felt the first time they told me that God said I was destined for greatness is extremely hard to explain, but it was like an electric shock to my system once the words were released. I squirmed in my seat as I sat at the kitchen table, my eyes begin to water, and the hair on my arms stood up. Those three words, "destined for greatness" were so powerful that it felt like fire ricocheting throughout my whole spirit. No one had ever previously spoken to me in this manner; it was as if she had just breathed life into my limp body.

Chapter Twelve

DESTINED FOR GREATNESS

I COULD NOT IGNORE THE feeling that felt like fire creeping through my bones, when those three words, *destined for greatness*, were spoken into my life. I knew from that point on; God had a special plan of my life.

I had made many decisions throughout my life, and most of them weren't good ones. I was used to being constantly reminded of all of the things that I did wrong—all the things I should have done, or could have done, but didn't do. No one had ever told me that despite everything else in my life that I was destined for greatness. It was definitely a new and different feeling. There was something in my godparent's eyes and something special about this unique awareness of a new and different life when they brought me home from the homeless shelter to a real home. Little did I know, that one affirmation would be the tiny seed planted to change the course of my life.

Despite the fact that I made bad choices, despite the fact that I was in a homeless shelter, despite the fact that my future didn't look bright, despite the fact that I was a high school dropout, they saw greatness in a troubled youth!

I had to put this story about the very first time I heard that I was destined for greatness in this book because it is important to know when you are destined for greatness. If you are going to accomplish anything in this life, you have to know that God has designed you to do it. You have to know that it's your destiny. You don't have to know everything; you just need to know that God destined you for this position in life! Your position may be becoming a business owner, leading a ministry, investing in real estate, building a school, doing something on an international basis, starting a restaurant, creating a food chain, directing day care centers, or having the capability of creating generational wealth. There are a great many possibilities for your position. So, whatever it is, know that you are destined to do it. I firmly believe God did not give you a desire that He will not develop!

From the time I was a little girl, I've always loved houses. I used to take a pen and paper or crayons and just draw houses for hours. I would draw streets with houses on it. I loved drawing big houses with a variety of different rooms, and I would make it a home with a front yard and back yard, complete with swings in the yard.

One day, my mother and I were going to the VA hospital in West Haven, Connecticut. On the side of the VA hospital, there was a group of properties in the process of being built. I must have had an expression or shown an interest so strong that my mother had asked if I wanted to go and see the houses. I'll never forget walking into the house. The house was not complete at all; in fact, it was just framed. There were no walls or floors, other than the plywood, no kitchen, no bathroom, or any light fixtures. However, when I walked into this unfinished house, I saw a finished product. I told my mother where the kitchen sink was going to go, where the toilet would go, where the light fixtures would go, and even where the chandelier would hang. It was all so very natural to me.

The love of houses was a desire that was deep within me even as a little girl. So, it should not have been a surprise when I started investing in real estate, when I opened my first real estate company, when I started my property management company, my real estate development company, or even my real estate school. Everything somehow came to full circle from my childhood love of houses, and ultimately, real estate—because it was destined.

When I talk about *being destined for greatness*, I talk about the destiny that is already prepared for you. I truly believe that we all have a destiny to fulfill. God did not just design us to occupy space until he comes. But He has designed us to make an impact on this world until He comes. Far too often, our destiny or life purpose gets lost in the day-to-day activities and the problems that plague us. However, when you know that you're destined for greatness, you even see the roadmap to your destiny through the problems that you encounter.

For example, if I would have never been a problem teenager that ended up being homeless, I wouldn't be writing this book, right now. I definitely wouldn't be right in the chapter entitled you're "destined for greatness." It was at my lowest time in a shelter that my greatest blessing showed its face in the form of my godparents. Little did they know that the positive affirmation they gave me would be just what I needed to fulfill my destiny.

Now, I have three children, and all three children will tell you the exact same thing; as long as they can remember, I have told them they are destined for greatness. I have also made them recite this positive affirmation over their own lives. I have made them say their name, and then state that they are destined for greatness. What this does is to command the atmosphere, and it speaks into the future—it speaks of faith; it speaks of endurance; it speaks of perseverance, and it speaks of God's hand on their lives.

You see, life is a fight. But if there is one thing that I know, it is you will never win a fight if you go into the battle thinking you're about to be defeated. You must enter the fight knowing that it doesn't matter what it looks like or feels like, but I'm destined for greatness, so I'm destined to win. I have never lost sight of the fact that I am on a divine assignment, and because of this assignment, I am destined for greatness. I understand that without the test, there is no testimony. When you take on life with a sense of confidence, you will win. It's just very unfortunate that many people were never taught how everything God has created is great—including themselves.

I have adopted the mindset of living "in purpose and on purpose;" coupled with the Scripture in Romans 8:31 (NIV) that reads: "What, then, shall we say in response to these things? If God is for us, who can be against us?" These two things, coupled together, have made me fearless. So fearless that I go after everything I believe God has for me. I eventually became so convinced that I was truly destined for greatness, and ultimately, I became so fearless that poverty had to bow down and be destroyed in my life.

Chapter Thirteen

MY HEART WAS POUNDING WITH one eye open and one eye closed; I anxiously waited on the result of the pregnancy test. Slowly one stripe appeared and then, the second stripe appeared—confirmation. Spoken softly, "I am pregnant," were my infamous words. So many thoughts ran across my mind—all at the same time.

What would my mother say? What would my mother do? Did I read the instructions wrong? What do these two stripes mean? I'm going to take this test again. Baby? But I'm a baby myself. I'm still in high school. Will I have to go to Polly McCabe school? What will my friends think? I can't party for nine months. What will my brother say? A baby, really? How will I take care of him or her?

My mom is going to put me out again. Where will my baby and I live? How am I going to tell the father? When should I tell him? What if he leaves us? I don't have a job. I can't support myself or a child. Baby, but I'm a baby about to have a baby. God, you have to take control of my life!

I put my left hand on my flat stomach as my right hand held the pregnancy test showing two stripes—one stripe representing me, and the other stripe representing the unborn child inside of me. I was overwhelmed with thoughts, but the one thought that gave me a sense of peace was that God is the creator of life. I began to think about all of the girls I knew who already had children. They seemed to be okay. *If they can do it, so can I*, I thought.

"I'm pregnant," I said randomly to my boyfriend as we drove down the street coming from getting ice cream. He stopped and pulled over to the side of the road. "Pregnant?" he said. "Yes," I pulled out the pregnancy test and showed it to him. I was nervous about his response. I wasn't sure what he would say or do. "Wow, okay," he said, then smiled and gave me a long hug. I didn't know what was going through his mind, but he seemed to be happy. He wasn't flustered at all. His happiness and calmness made me feel at ease.

Almost immediately, he had me move in with him. We temporarily stayed on Rosette Street in the house where he and his partner were running their drug operations. During this time, there wasn't a shortage of money. He purchased everything I wanted, and I mean everything! For my birthday, he purchased me a brand-new powder Blue Nissan Mirage Coupe. I drove the car off the lot with zero miles!

When I became eight months pregnant, we moved into our apartment, which was located on the third-floor on Elm Street in New Haven. There was a convenience store on the first floor of our apartment building, and I was always thankful for it when I needed to pick up an item or two, such as milk and eggs.

The apartment we lived in had only the best. We had a black lacquer eight seat dining room table with a custom beveled mirror top. I accessorized it with custom hunter green and pink floral placemats to match the custom hunter green and pink floral drapes. This is during the 1990s, so of course, we had a waterbed and a faux leather living room set.

Our apartment was so nice that the landlord would use it as a model apartment when he had a vacancy. I kept the apartment immaculate, but it didn't stop the legion of roaches from swarming in as soon as the lights went out. You can categorize our life as "ghetto-fabulous".

I gained sixty pounds with my pregnancy. I felt like I was going to literally burst any minute. I never thought I would go from weighing 125 pounds to weighing 185 pounds in less than nine months. I was told that the average weight gain was between twenty and twenty-five pounds, and this is what I expected, but as I learned early on with most things in my life, nothing went as expected.

I was a week overdue. I could barely move, but my unborn child couldn't keep still! It was amazing to look at God's work. My stomach was constantly moving and changing shapes. One moment, my stomach would look completely round, then the next minute, my stomach was lower on the right and significantly higher on the left. Then, lower on the left and significantly higher on the right. I'll never forget the strong, persistent kick that was also very visible. Yes, a perfect round stomach with a foot visible on the side! It was wonderful to experience God's first-hand work of bringing life into this world.

I had heard all of the stories of how labor was God's curse to women for disobeying Him in the Garden of Eden. I was also told that labor pain would be the worst pain I would ever feel in my life-time. However, being a week overdue, I was ready to go into labor and get the baby out of me.

The doctors suggested I do more walking to help induce my labor. So, I walked, walked, and walked, or should I say wobbled, wobbled, and wobbled! The doctors were right; all of the walking finally paid off. My son's father and I went to "The Jump," a local club located on Winchester Avenue in New Haven. God is definitely in the timing. The club closed at 2:00 a.m. and my contractions started at 2:00 a.m. on May 1st. By the time he got to me, ten min-utes later, it was time to go to the hospital.

I certainly wasn't feeling the Braxton Hicks contractions; these were the REAL THING! No guessing was needed. It was time to give birth. On the way to Yale-New Haven Hospital, I called my mom to let her know I was in labor. I don't know how she got to the hospital before me, but she did. It was something very comforting to have my mother in the delivery room with me. This was the day I realized that just maybe, my mom loved me.

And yes, what I was told was very much true. This was the worst pain I have ever felt! I screamed at the top of my lungs for the doctors to give me pain medicine. Prior to delivery, my doctor and I had discussed the types of pain medicine for labor and the side effects. I was well prepared mentally for the pain, and I knew that if it became unbearable, all I had to do was ask for the pain medicine. So, as soon as the nurses positioned me on the bed, and the contractions started coming, I screamed, "pain medicine!"

The nurses were ready to give me the pain medicine to take me out of the agony when my doctor said, "No, this birth has to be done naturally. It's too late." Yes, my son was on his way into the world. At this time, all I had was my God, my mom, and the pushing. Less than two hours later, Dante, my baby boy, had entered into this world.

The little blue hospital hat could barely fit on his head. He was in my birthing canal for an extended time, and the shape of his head mimicked a cone. The little blue hat balanced on his head, and as a new mom, I was concerned. But the doctors assured me he was okay and that his head would take its natural shape.

My grandmother quickly gave me the old school remedy of how to shape a newborn's head. So, I did just what my grandmother taught me, and I began shaping his little head. I'm not sure if the doctors were correct in telling me to do nothing, or if my grandmother was correct in having me to shape his head, but after a few weeks, he had a perfectly round head.

He was so tiny, but he was still bigger than the other babies in the nursery. I watched him through the glass window with the other newborn babies. I looked at him and marveled at the way he moved in the hospital bassinet.

"Do you want me to bring your baby to you?" a nurse asked as she was walking into the nursery. "Yes, please. Baby Hoskie." She looked at my wrist to confirm my name and continued inside the nursery and pushed my son out to me. I pushed him to my room and lined his bassinet up next to my bed. I got into the bed, laid on my right side facing my baby boy, who was bundled up so tight, and I watched him through the clear bassinet while he peacefully slept.

I took a deep breath, closed my eyes, and felt the absolute gift of pure love for the very first time in my life. A strong love—one that I never knew existed until I laid eyes on him. A love between a mother and child. This new-found mother's love made me question the way I thought of my mother. Up until this point, I really thought my mom didn't love me. My thoughts had clearly changed since I had become a new mother. I thought... *How can it be possible that my mom doesn't love me? ...Maybe, I was wrong all of these years. Maybe, my mom did love me. Maybe, she just didn't know how to express it.*

I knew the love I felt for my child was deeply rooted, and it came from God. So, it just made sense to me that the same thing would have happened to her when I was born. This was the day that God, not only showed me what love was but He restored it—between my mom and me.

Chapter Fourteen

LIFE WAS GOOD, AND I didn't have to worry about one bill. My son's father purchased everything my son needed. Stacks of money were everywhere, and we were all set for life. However, the Barbie and Ken fairytale quickly came to an end. My son's father began being manipulative and controlling, then physically abusive. Anytime he was under the influence; he would beat me with his fist or anything he could find nearby.

"Stop, stop, stop, please, stop!" I begged because I was scared for my life. He picked up an old-fashioned mop with the metal clamp to hold the mop head in place and began swinging and beating me. I backed myself into the kitchen corner and slid down the wall, hiding my face in my knees with my arms covering my head. I couldn't beat a 220-pound, six-foot-one man, who was under the influence.

I thought he would stop when he saw me in a vulnerable position, but he didn't. He continued to beat me with the mop until the metal piece made a deep cut in my left arm and blood gushed out and smeared all over the white kitchen floor. The sight of blood must have interrupted his high because he stopped in mid-swing when he finally noticed the puddle of blood. "I'm sorry, Punkin', I'm sorry," he muttered. I got up and ran out of the apartment as fast as I could. I ran down the stairs as if my life depended on it, which it did.

The neighbors must have heard me screaming for my life and called the police. As I was running outside with a black eye and a bloody arm, the police were running up the stairs on their way to my apartment. The officer looked at me, and said in a stern voice, "Ma'am what's going on? Are you okay?" I immediately stopped in my tracks because I was scared of my boyfriend—scared of what would happen if I told the police. So, I smiled and held my head up, looked the officer straight in the eye, and said, "Yes, officer, everything is okay. Thanks for asking," I said in a shaky voice. I'm sure they saw right through me. They probably saw a young girl abused and trapped.

I knew if I was to press charges, and my son's father had to go to jail for abusing me; then there would be no financial support for myself and my son. Of course, he would constantly remind me that I had nothing without him. The sad thing is it was the truth. I had nothing—absolutely nothing. Without his support, I couldn't afford the designer clothes that I was wearing. I certainly couldn't pay the rent, buy groceries, pay the car note, or even buy gas for the car. I had absolutely nothing without him. I wanted to leave, but I felt suffocated and trapped with no way whatsoever out.

I would imagine leaving him in the middle of the night while he was sleeping. I even went so far as to pack a small bag of clothes as I planned my escape from this abusive relationship. Then reality showed its ugly face. I didn't want to go back to a state of homelessness. I couldn't fathom the thought of going back into a shelter, especially with a baby. I knew that things wouldn't get better, but deep down inside, I felt as if I had no means of escape.

At first, I didn't notice it when it was happening, but slowly and surely, he alienated me from my friends and family, so I had no one to turn to and nowhere to go. I never knew what to expect from him. One moment, he was the perfect boyfriend, and the next, he was the boyfriend straight from hell. I became very emotionally shattered.

I was at a state where I just couldn't take anymore. I was consumed with the thoughts of what I was going to do the next time he decided to start beating me again. I would imagine me taking objects, hitting him right in the head, and even stabbing him in his sleep. This was just too much abuse, and I had had enough.

The abuse was getting out of control. I thought it was my secret, but evidently, I was mistaken. We were out with a group of friends, playing the role of the "perfect couple," when he raised his hand to get something that was behind me, and I jumped from fear in front of everyone.

One of the girls with us pulled me aside privately and said, "I heard he was beating on you, but I didn't believe it until just now when I saw you jump." Of course, I denied it. "No, that's crazy, people are always talking and don't know what they are talking about," I said defensively. But she gave me a look as if she knew I was lying. I twisted my lips to the left, raised my right eyebrow, and turned my head to the side as to say... *Now, get the heck out of my face.* I went back and sat next to my son's father, hugged up in his arms, laughing with the crowd, and smiling on the outside while embarrassed and crying on the inside.

I would always know when a fight was about to happen. He would always start the same way by accusing me of cheating on him. One day, he said that he heard me on the telephone talking to a man, and I hung up as soon as he walked in the door. This was the furthest from the truth. I wasn't even on the phone.

I knew what was coming next. But this time, I had had enough! I wasn't going to take the beatings anymore. I was ready to fight, and I did! We went back and forth, punch by punch, and blow by blow. He pulled back to hit me, and I pulled back to hit him. I was fighting him as if I were back in high school fighting a girl that was just talking too much junk. He went to grab me, and I bent down, grabbed his legs, picked him up—all 220 pounds—and slammed him on our mirror coffee table! The table immediately shattered into hundreds of pieces all over the living room. Both of his hands were cut and both of his arms. Now, he was all bloody. He couldn't take seeing his own blood, and now he was screaming for help.

My, oh, my. How good it felt to see the "tables" turned.

Eventually, the abuse died down, but it never ended. I just learned how to fight back, so he knew what to expect when he hit me—tit for tat—a hit back! The fact that I was still financially trapped had plagued me. I had nothing going for myself. When I looked at my future, I couldn't see anything. I had no vision or plan for my life. I knew I had to do better. Otherwise, I would forever be financially dependent, and it didn't make me feel good about myself. I had to do something—and soon.

My son's father had slowed down selling drugs since his partner had recently been arrested, and he feared the authorities would come for him next. The lack of finances will bring stress to any relationship, but it brought about massive stress and upgraded abuse. Here I was a teenage mother in an abusive relationship with the self-esteem level of zero and now broke!

Chapter Fifteen

"I'M NOT LEAVING HERE... WE have nowhere to go," I said, as I rocked back and forth in the chair, holding my son in my arms tightly with tears falling down my face. *"I've applied for over a hundred apartments, and I keep getting denied. They keep saying that $417 per month isn't enough, but it's all I got! This is it, $417, and I'll give it all to you. We can eat from food stamps. I'll just write my check to you. Please, Ma'am, please Ma'am. I'm begging you because we have nowhere to go."*

I was at a breaking point. I finally got the courage to leave my son's father, but I had nothing. "I'm sorry, Miss. Hoskie, the property manager, Arlene, isn't here and we don't have any vacancies. You can fill out this paperwork to be put on our waiting list," she said as she handed me the clipboard. "How long is the waiting list?" I asked. "It's hard to tell. There have been people on the list for over three years, but it depends on the level of hardship. If the person is handicapped or disabled, they take priority over other people on the list," she explained in a calm rehearsed tone.

"Three years, Ma'am. You don't understand, we have NOWHERE to go," I said, with my eyes closed, rocking my son in my arms and tears still flowing down my face. "You may want to go to Life Haven; it's a family shelter on Ferry Street in New Haven. They may have room for you and your son." "I'm not taking him to a shelter; I just can't. Please, help me. I was told that your organization had apartments that went according to your income. They told me to ask for Lyndell Harp, and he would help me. I'm enrolled at Gateway College, and I'm going to get an internship at Yale University. I just need an opportunity to get on my feet; that's all I'm asking for—an opportunity."

I couldn't stop crying. I was all out of options. No one would give me an apartment, and the thought of being homeless with my son made me feel like a complete failure. I had made up my mind that I wasn't taking my son to a shelter. However, I didn't know how I was going to stop it from happening, but I knew I had to—somehow.

"Ms. Hoskie, again, Mr. Harp isn't available and the Property Manager, Arlena handles the rentals and she isn't here. Again, you can sign-up for our waiting list," she said, as she picked the clipboard up again and handed it to me. I took the clipboard and sat it on the table next to me.

"Listen, lady, I'm trying to be respectful, and I don't think you are hearing me. I HAVE NOWHERE TO GO. Period." I was doing everything mentally to not turn my desperation into anger. A wise person told me that when you want someone to do something for you that you would attract more "bees with honey than you would with lemons". So, I was on my best behavior.

I had been catching buses while looking for apartments faithfully every single day of the week for three whole months. My mother allowed me and my son to sleep on her couch in the den. We had all of our belongings in a black trash bag, which sat in the corner next to the couch. My mother made it very clear that we had only three months to stay with her before we would have to find an alternative place to live.

Every other day, my mother would remind me by asking, "How's your apartment search going?" She had put me out in the past, so I knew she was definitely serious this time. It was different now, but before when I didn't have anywhere to stay, I would just hang out at a friend's house late and "accidentally" fall asleep. I did this on numerous occasions while growing up. I was living from couch-to-couch. However, things were different now; I can't get away with that trick with having my son. What if he wakes up in the middle of the night and wants to play with his trucks? Or he's hungry? I needed for him to have stability in his life.

Often when I looked at my son, I felt like I was letting him down. He didn't ask for me as a mother. I couldn't even provide shelter for him. I felt unfit to care for my child. I bowed my head, held my son close, and I prayed with all of my heart, right in the lobby of the Property Management office. I didn't care who saw me crying. I went from silent tears streaming down my face to bawling my eyes out. I was beyond desperate.

> *Father, I need You right now. I'm helpless. I'm hopeless. I'm trying all I know, but Father nothing is working. Please, Father, please, I'm begging You. Please, don't allow us to go into a shelter. Help me provide for him God; I need You now more than ever before. I have nothing but hope in You. But I was taught that hope in God is enough. You gave me my son, and I'm unfit to be his mom. I'm trying Father. I just can't do it alone; I need You…*

Just then, I felt a hand rubbing the right side of my back to console me. "Miss. Hoskie," she said in a pleasant, compassionate voice. I looked up, a bit startled from being in deep prayer. An African American woman with a light, caramel complexion and a short curly afro that reminded me of a Jheri curl and glasses stood over me. "My name is Arlenea. I'm the Property Manager here, let's go talk at my desk," she said. She had gone on a cigarette break and saw me in the lobby when she returned. She cleared the middle of her desk by moving the piles of papers to the right and left sides of the desk.

God answered my prayer that day.

He gave Arlenea a heart of compassion at that very moment, and somehow, I became a priority over all of the people on the three-year waiting list. I was given my first apartment. It was a two-bedroom apartment with heat and hot water included for $79 per month because the rent was according to my income. I sat in her office as tears flowed down my eyes as she prepared the paperwork. As fast as I could wipe a tear, another one would fall down. But now my tears were transformed for tears hurt to tears of joy.

Now, I was crying because God heard my cry.

Chapter Sixteen

LIFE WAS GOOD; I WAS all set! I had my apartment, my welfare check, food stamps, and I was enrolled in the WIC program (Women, Infants & Children). The WIC program provided vouchers for free milk, cheese, juice, and beans. I felt a real sense of independence when I received my public assistance check and WIC vouchers. I know it seems as if I were in a low place, but this was a financial level higher than what I was accustomed to living. At least, the check and vouchers were in my name. It felt good to have control over my own money even if it was welfare money. I no longer had to ask anyone for money—my son's father or be a financial burden to anyone—I had my own.

I looked forward to getting the check of $417.00 faithfully in the mail on the third of every month. There were times where I planned my entire day around getting my check. I knew the mailman by name, along with everyone else in the community.

The mailman would deliver mail by 3 p.m., but on the third of the month, our "payday," he managed to get our checks to us a little earlier than on an average mail day. He understood that he was serving a community of people, who were definitely dependent on their state checks. He also was well aware that it would be a huge problem if he didn't deliver the checks on time for us to make it to the bank. On "payday," the mailman was either our best friend or our worse enemy.

The poverty mindset plagued everything around me, and I didn't even notice it. I had friends whose parents had taught them by example. They were taught that if they wanted more money from the State, then they needed to have another child. Yes, another child and everyone was popping out children for an additional $150 per month, plus increased food stamps.

No one was talking about bettering themselves with education, owning a business, signing your own paycheck, investing in the Stock Market, investing in real estate, creating multiple streams of income, or even striving for a good job. We were in the "hood," and the focus was on how to maximize your State benefits and who were meeting up at the "Jump," the local club, for the free fried chicken wings on Tuesdays!

As idiotic as this sounds, unfortunately, it was the "norm," and during this time, I didn't see anything wrong with it. Everyone was cashing in on the welfare checks. Since the rent of the apartment went according to our income, the cost of living was low, and it would appear as if we had it made in a welfare-dependent world.

Why strive for more when your rent is paid, food is on the table, clothes are on you back, and you didn't have to do anything to live this lifestyle. Everyone was doing the same thing, and that was absolutely nothing!

*****

Ring, ring, "Hi Mom," I said. "You should come with me tonight; there is a guest preacher coming into town, and he's preaching right around the corner from where you live," my mother said to me over the phone. "Sure, what time?" I said. "At the 7 p.m. service. I'll be at your house at 6:55 p.m.," my mother responded. "Okay, Diege and I will be ready when you come to pick us up." My son's nickname, Diege, was given to him by one of his father's friends, Tonya, who walked into the living room one day and said with a loud voice, "Hi ya, Diege!" Little did she know, but she had just renamed my son.

I hung up the phone with my mom and began getting myself and my son ready to go to church with my mom. "Come here, Diege, let mommy put the drops in your ear." Diege never liked getting the ear medicine. He had chronic ear infections, so the doctors had prescribed three drops in his left ear per day. I put this ear drop doses on a schedule of one drop every four hours during the day.

My mom pulled up outside at 6:55 on the dot in her dark gray Hyundai with the red line that went around the entire car. She had purchased it a couple of years prior—brand-new off the lot. She later found out that the salesman, who was a family member, had scammed her out of some money since she overpaid for the car. Nevertheless, it was reliable transportation and much better than the vehicle she had before this car.

We pulled up to the "mom and pop" church and couldn't find a parking space. The closest parking space was four blocks away. *This guy must be a good preacher,* I thought to myself. The Spirit of God was definitely present in that church. It reminded me of my god-father's church. The organist was ushering God's spirit in, and the people were praising God. Some were slain in the Spirit, some were dancing, some singing, and others were speaking in tongues.

Diege was well-behaved but very curious during the service. He was always a quiet child and never gave me any problems. He kept standing on my lap to get a good view of what was going on in the building. He was absorbing the atmosphere and what was going on like a little computer. I tried to sit him down, and he would stand back up. This kept going on until I gave up and just let him see what was going on.

"If you are here and you want special prayer, come and join the line forming on the left," the preacher said. My mother immediately stood up to get in the line and motioned for me to join her. So, I picked up Diege, put him on my right hip, and stood in the prayer line.

It looked like everyone in the building was in the prayer line. We had about thirty people ahead of us and even more behind us waiting for prayer. I began to get hot all over, and not because someone had turned up the thermostat. I felt God's Spirit, and I knew He was trying to get my attention. I knew that when it was my time to get prayer, I had to listen attentively to what the preacher was saying. Diege was still taking in the environment and watching the people praise God like he was in an amusement park. He couldn't stay still, looking from right to left and left to right. Perhaps, he felt God's presence, as well.

I was just watching all of the people before me, fall slain in the Spirit—one-by-one. I was next, and I was determined not to hit the floor like everybody else. But I was ready for the message; the preacher was about to deliver to me. I walked up slowly with Diege on my right hip and my left hand in the air. "Ushers come get her baby for her," he said in a fast voice. They ran over and carefully took my son out of my arms. The preacher put anointing oil on his right hand, placed his hand on my forehand while I raised both of my hands, and he began to speak, "My daughter, you have a great purpose in God's Kingdom and so does your son. The enemy is keeping you distracted, but I cause you, daughter, this day to rise."

He motioned for the usher to bring my son to him. He placed his hand on my son's head and then moved it to his left ear and prayed, "Father, I cause a healing of his hearing, right now. I cause your miracle-working power to let loose on this child and heal him from all of his infirmity." My little slanted eyes opened wide with surprise because there was no way he could have known about my son's chronic ear infections. There weren't any tubes coming from his ear, and he couldn't tell I had put ear drops in the same ear he was praying over just hours prior. So, I knew this man was working in God's power. He looked back at me, eye-to-eye, pointing at my son, and said the words that would forever change the way I looked at life. The preacher said, "His life is directly linked to your life. Whatever you do will impact his future." He laid his hands on my forehead, and I hit the church floor—slain in the Spirit.

Chapter Seventeen

HIS LIFE LINKED TO MY life. It sounded simple enough. However, it was far from simple. This one statement had caused me to re-evaluate everything around me. It had caused me to look at the woman in the mirror and then be honest with her. Was I where I wanted to be in life? Was I happy? Was I fulfilled? Was I financially stable? And most of all, what would my son's life be like if it were "linked to mine?"

When I was honest with myself, I finally realized that my life was a mess! No matter how much people around me seemed like they were living the life on welfare in the hood. I knew, if my son's life was linked to mine in my current situation, I would cause him to fail at life. I would cause him to repeat the same poverty behaviors, which would cause impoverished results.

For the first time in my life, I realized poverty had a stronghold over my life, and to make matters worse, I was accepting it. Yes, I accepted it because it was all I knew. I accepted it because everyone around me made it seem like fun. Fun, not to have to work hard, fun to collect a welfare check, and fun to have your rent paid by the state. But when I looked at where I was bringing my son, the love of my life; I saw nothing positive, and it wasn't fun anymore.

I saw my life linked with his, but I saw his life worse than mine. He was a Black male born in the '90s with a father, who was a drug dealer, and a mother, who was a high school dropout. I had lost numerous friends to the streets throughout the years, and I had been in the midst of gang violence on several occasions.

I continued to evaluate my life and go down memory lane. I remembered how my life was speared on Edgewood Avenue, years prior. I was in a car with my friends, who had been in a street war with the guys from Winchester Avenue. I sat behind the driver's seat during the shoot-out. Not only was the car shot up, but so were the people in it. The guy in the passenger seat and the driver were shot while the guy sitting next to me in the back seat was shot twice.

So, I jumped up from my trip down memory lane with a determination that my son, would not be a product of the environment I had created for him. I knew that his life depended on it, and I was not going to fail him. I was determined not to lose my son to the streets, to the jail cells, and especially not to gang violence. I had to figure a way out for his life.

At the moment, I was clueless. I had no idea how I was going to break the poverty cycle. I just knew I had to do something to break the cycle because the statistics were stacked against him in large negative proportions. Suddenly, my education became my priority, and the people around me became less important.

I enrolled at Gateway Community College year-round—no summers off for me, to accomplish my new goals. I became focused. I was no longer looking forward to going to the club for the free chicken wings. Now, I was home studying and teaching my son how to read. We would do homework together. This was my way of entertaining him while I had real homework to do. I would pull out my books, and I would give him his Dr. Seuss books, Crayola Crayons, and blank paper. When I was finished, he would be finished, and we would give ourselves a treat—chocolate chip cookies and milk.

There were no excuses—not one was acceptable at this time in my life. I had extreme focus. On many occasions, I didn't have a babysitter, but that didn't keep me at home or cause me to miss class. I packed up my baby boy with his books, crayons, and paper with his very own backpack, and we went to school together. I would set him up in the back of the classroom with his toys and snacks, go to my seat, and act like everything was normal. My teachers never complained; they too, acted like this was normal. I was focused because my baby boy's life depended on it. Rain, hail, or snow storm—it didn't matter. My son and I were at the bus stop on the corner of

Shelton and Division Street catching the "G" bus to transfer to the "Z" bus so that I could get to school.

When it was brutally cold, I made sure I dressed him warm. He had on long johns, shirt, pants, a sweater, two pairs of socks, a snowsuit, a coat, a hat that tied underneath his chin to be sure his ears were covered, and then last, but not least, I covered his face with Vaseline. By the time I was finished dressing him, he could barely move, but he wasn't going to be cold.

Diege enjoyed the bus rides as he got to stand in the seat and look out of the window while the bus road through different neighborhoods. "No, Ma," Diege said as he shook his head profusely backing up from the opened front door. "Caaaar," he pointed to the cars driving down the street. "Yes, honey, car," I replied, thinking he was trying to learn vocabulary. I reached for his hand to walk out the door. "No, Ma, no," Diege repeatedly said while refusing to leave the house. "Caaaar." "Yes, honey, car. Now, let's go catch the bus."

Diege, began to cry. Then, I realized he didn't like going outside in the cold, and he didn't like the bus as much as I thought he did. "Mommy doesn't have a car, but I will, Son." I squatted down to look at him face-to-face to assure him that someday, Mommy will have a car. I gave him a big hug, picked him up, and ran to the bus stop so that we didn't miss it. We caught the bus, Diege stood on the seats, looked out of the window, and continued to point at the cars.

"I will have a car, one day, but right now, the buses are getting too expensive," I said to myself. I had just finished dumping out all of my pocketbooks for the change to pay for the bus I was going to ride. I made it a habit to pick up change wherever I would find it to save for the bus rides. The little push back that I received from my son made me go into deep thought.

Look at all of the people with cars, I thought.

Up until then, I hadn't even thought about purchasing a car. The thought just never crossed my mind.

Chapter Eighteen

HEAVILY SEDATED…BEEP, BEEP, BEEP, BEEP… I heard the sound from the hospital monitor. My eyes opened and closed—continuously for several minutes. I could hear doctors speaking in the background. "We may need to do a blood transfusion. She has lost a lot of blood." In the distance, I could hear the sound of high heels running down the hospital hallway…the sound was getting closer and closer.

"I'm her mother; let me in." I lifted my head to see my mother pulling back the hospital curtain. She was breathing heavily with a look of serious concern. As she rubbed my forehand, moving my hair out of the way, she began praying. "Satan, I come to serve notice that you must flee in seven different directions! In the name of Jesus, no weapon you form against my child shall prosper. Satan, you cannot have my child; she belongs to God! I command you to lose your hold, right now. The blood of Jesus is against you! Father, restore, restore, right now!" She continued to pray firmly over me and speak in other tongues—discreetly so that the doctors didn't hear her voice.

"Mom, am I going to die?" Before I could continue, she blurted, "No! You're my child," she said with great authority and stern faith. The sternness of her voice gave me a feeling of peace that God would not allow me to die because of her relationship with him.

The doctors couldn't get my hemorrhaging to stop. They were gathered around the outside of the curtain discussing their next move while my mother was on the other side, binding the devil and calling on Jesus. On the inside of the curtain, I was scared for my life. My body was out of control, and there was nothing I could do while everything the doctors performed, thus far, just wasn't working.

"Father, forgive me for my sins, and my shortcomings. God have mercy on me. Please, Father, have mercy," I prayed within my spirit.

Whatever my fate, it rested in the hands of God. When it came down to whom I wanted to be with me during this sad moment in my life, I didn't call my friends, and I didn't call my boyfriend. Instead, I called my mama! She was the first person I thought of when the complications began. I gave the doctor my mother's phone number and asked them to call her. All of our indifferences we had in the past didn't seem to matter at that moment. I was scared for my life, I needed Mama, and she was right there.

The curtains opened, and a male doctor in his forties wearing an all-white three-quarter length jacket with light royal blue scrubs stood on the side of the bed with a clipboard in his hand and looking at his notes. *"We are going to wait another thirty minutes to see if the bleeding slows down. If it doesn't, we will have to give her a blood transfusion. We don't want her to lose too much more blood,"* he said as he looked at my mother. "May I have a word with you?" my mother asked. "Sure, as long as Roberta gives consent. We have HIPPA laws that I must follow concerning a patient's confidentiality," he said as he looked at me. Although I didn't want to, there was no way I would say no. So, I nodded my head to indicate yes, and said, "You can talk to her."

My mother walked on the other side of the curtains, and he followed. I couldn't hear all of the questions that my mother was asking. However, what I did know was that as soon as he answered one question of her questions, she had another question immediately following. She was going to make sure the doctors were doing their part and was making the best decisions concerning the next steps for me. After she got a clear understanding of what was going on with me, she came back on the other side of the curtain, laid her hands back on my forehand and proceeded to pray, again.

I laid helplessly in the bed. The medication made me sleepy. I kept dozing on and off. I was desperately trying to stay awake, but the medication was winning the battle. I fell into a deep sleep, and the next thing I knew, I was being discharged without any further medical procedures.

On that day, I thanked God for my praying mother. She got her prayers through, and God had answered them. God was mending our broken mother/daughter relationship. After becoming a mother, I had viewed my relationship with my own mother much differently. Yes, we had our challenges, but I understood that despite it all, she did still love me. She may not have expressed the actual words "I love you," but I was mature enough to watch her actions, and her actions told it all. When my back was against the wall, I knew who would come to my rescue without question or doubt—it was Mama.

During this time, I had made a conscientious effort to put our relationship in perspective. As people, we can only give what we have inside of us to give. Maybe, I was looking for something that wasn't inside of her. I'm sure her relationship with her mother played a role in how she raised her children. I believe she did the best she knew how to do. I believe she was a better mom to me than her mom was to her.

I found out that we were more alike than we were the opposite. We are both very analytical, particular, and have a dry sense of humor. We are both serious about living right for God and believe in interceding for people. We would give our last to someone in need, but we will cut you off quick if we're taken for granted. If we have a choice to eat breakfast, lunch, or dinner, we would both choose breakfast. We both have little tolerance when things don't go our way, and that may be one of the reasons our personalities had clashed in my teenage years. It has been said that the reason some mother/daughter or father/son relationships don't make it is because they are too much alike. Maybe, just maybe, there may be some truth to that belief.

I didn't want to have a conversation with my mother about how I ended up in the hospital, but I knew there was no way I could avoid it. I was nineteen, living on my own, so I was considered grown. However, I didn't want to let her down with my actions. My mother and I got on the elevator to go home. I was completely silent. As soon as the elevator doors closed, and we were alone, my mother said. "That was my baby, too. I deserved to know."

Chapter Nineteen

MY DADDY'S HOME

I STARED IN AMAZEMENT. ACTUALLY, in awe at the way his hands moved so smoothly over the piano. He performed a melody that had all of the family mesmerized and locked into his solo rendition. *Wow*, I thought, I never knew that the part of me I gave up after my grandfather died wasn't even given to me by my grandfather.

As a little girl, I loved playing the piano and organ. My grandfather taught me how to play the song, *Jesus Build a Fence Around Me* on the old organ my mother had. I played so well as a child; I had even learned to play *Here Comes the Bride* for my cousin's wedding. When my grandfather passed, I vowed not to play the organ anymore because this was something, I thought, was a part of him in me—until this Thanksgiving Day performance by my dad.

There he sat, playing the piano, singing the songs he had written and was the life of the party. It had been eleven years since I had seen him, but Harvey was home from Georgia. So, the family treated him as if he had never left. I listened and watched him with mixed emotions. Happy to be in my dad's presence; yet, mad because he had abandoned me for eleven long years. I was even confused because he had never apologized. Did he really think that leaving his family for years with no support was acceptable and it didn't warrant an apology?

Nevertheless, Daddy was home, and I chose to be happy for the moment. I suppose he tried to be a father and make up for the past by being my dedicated babysitter. I no longer had to take Diege to school with me. My father would take pride in watching his grandson.

Harvey was living in a rooming house, and everyone in the apartment building knew his grandson. There were seen and unseen problems. It was clear he was in an emotional battle with his mind. He returned home to Connecticut after falling from a ladder while painting a woman's house, and the fall had crushed his knees. Due to this accident, the doctors diagnosed that he was unable to work again. Harvey may not have had the best-paying jobs, but he had always kept a job. He never was the kind of man who asked for anything.

As far as I knew, his father, Dellie Hoskie, was a good father and role model. His father had been a Holiness Preacher, who taught his boys to be hard workers. My grandfather did his best in raising his boys to be men, but you know what they say about the PK's (Preacher's Kids), "The devil has it out for them." My father would always speak highly of his father and had never uttered a negative word about him.

I'll never forget the conversation I had with my dad about his father. "Dad was a Holiness Preacher. He didn't play with God," my father said. He continued, "Dad, didn't put up with no mess. He made sure his boys would work. Daddy made us all work at the Steel Mill with him. He said he wasn't raising no lazy men." My father had always talked about his father with great pride, and I just sat and listened.

"Dad took me, Eddie, Dellie, James, and Joseph out to the Canteen and sat us down, and told us, 'Boys, when you become a man there are three things you must always do, and that's the three Ps; Produce, Protect, and Provide. If you produce a child, you protect them, and provide for them.'"

My dad had smiled proudly as he went down the memory lane of his younger days while being raised by his dad. It was nice to hear about my grandfather trying his best to help his sons to be good men by teaching them about the three Ps. But I wondered if my father ever evaluated how well he did with the three Ps. I wondered if it bothered him at all that he only did one of the three P's and that was produced. I surely wasn't protected by him, and my mom had provided for me.

Not being able to work contributed to Harvey's drinking problem, and ultimately, his secret addiction. It wasn't long before his life went in a downward spiral. He would become extremely intoxicated, slurring his words, not able to stand up or think in a logical manner. One morning around 9 a.m., I needed to go to the corner store to get some milk for breakfast, I opened my front door to be greeted with my father completely passed out on my front porch, next to an old beat up Stop and Shop grocery cart filled with dirty plastic bottles— he had collected from the garbage.

"Dad, Dad!" I screamed. My heart had sunk as I began to imagine the worst. "Dad, Dad," I screamed again, but this time, I was shaking him with no response at all from him. I ran to call 911, but before I could dial the last one, he woke up. "Punkin' Nickel, Dad came to say hi," he said with one eye halfway open, and the other closed while attempting to roll over on his left side to get comfortable on my front porch. It was clear; he must have slept on my porch through the night. Dad may have been drunk, but this was a different type of "high" that I hadn't seen before.

His addictions grew worse over time, and he was in and out of the hospital for a heart condition that he had kept a secret from everyone. Eventually, my brother found Dad dead in his apartment. The doctors said his death was due to cardiac failure, but I couldn't help but wonder if the heart attack was induced by his non-alcoholic secret addictions. This was a shocking surprise to the family. Dad was only fifty-nine when he suddenly passed.

God had to deal with me about forgiving my father after he passed away. I was angry with him because he was dead. Yes, it is possible to hold negative emotion in your heart for people who are no longer living. I was angry at my dad because I felt that he chose his addiction over his family. I felt things could have been different if he would have tried harder to get clean, and if he truly loved his family, he would have put forth a stronger effort.

I'm no expert on addictions, but this is my opinion. I don't know what it's like to be addicted, but I know that it is possible to break any habit or stronghold. It took prayer and transparency with myself to realize: one, I was angry with him even though he was dead; and two, I had to forgive him even in his death as the Lord has forgiven me.

—*Take a moment and evaluate your heart, unforgiveness may be blocking your blessing and keeping you in bondage.*

Chapter Twenty

A LETTER OF REDEMPTION

Dear Ms. Hoskie,

It has been recommended to our office that you participate in our new Job Placement collaboration between Gateway Community College and Yale University. We have read your letters of recommendation, and the Board has unanimously agreed that you meet all of the qualifications to be approved for our program. You have been scheduled to meet with Yale University Human Resource Department to complete your placement process.

I HAD NO IDEA, WHICH professor(s) secretly recommended me to the placement program, but I was shaking while reading the letter I had received. I'm sure my instructor's heart went out for me when they would see me in class with my son. I was in class early to get my son situated. I made honors, and I never gave excuses. There were times that I had to bring his dinner to class. I would bring a blanket that I would set up in the corner for him to sit on to eat and play while I was focused on learning. I was told that if I did well in the program, there was a possibility that Yale may hire me permanently. An ounce of hope was all I needed. I had made up my mind, on the day I received the good news of my internship, that I would work hard, and it would become a permanent job.

I didn't forget that my son's life was directly linked to mine. He was the reason I worked so hard to better myself, and it felt good knowing that my labor and years of sacrifice were not in vain. God truly had used the professor or professors to bless me secretly and to open a door in my life, which would lead to the beginning of a new life for my son and me.

I had one more semester before graduating with my Associates Degree from Gateway Community College. I was happy to have been selected to do an internship at Yale University sorting mail. I took pride in sorting the mail. I was the best mail sorter that $9.14 per hour could hire. The mail was picked up early, sorted early, and I was finished early. "Is there anything else I can do in the office? I finished sorting the mail," I said to Lisa, the Department Administrator. "Are you finished already?" she said in a doubtful tone as she walked to the mailroom to check the mail cart confirming that the mail had been sorted. When she saw that my work was completed, she turned and said, "Wow, that was fast." She asked the Administrative Assistant to give me paperwork to file. Once again, I was focused and had finished filing in record time.

This time, I strategically, bypassed the Administrative Assistant and went to the Department Administrator and asked, "Is there anything else I can do in the office? I finished filing the paperwork that was given to me." Lisa looked puzzled and said, "Are you done already?" "Yes," I responded. She got up from her desk and went to where the large pile of papers were to see that they were filed. "That's pretty amazing, and you're fast," she said.

What the administrator didn't know was that I was given an opportunity to change my life, and I was going to give it 110percent of my effort. There were other employees in the Business Office, but I was focused on pleasing Lisa since she was the person in the position to hire and promote me. After a few weeks, of consistent hard work, I was permanently hired.

Now, I had my first real job! Life was getting better for my son and me, but I was far from content. I was hungry for life and all of the challenges it had for me. Getting my first real job was confirmation that hard work and focus pays off. Just how far life would take me was yet to be seen.

Chapter Twenty-One

I WAS THANKFUL FOR THE program and the job. So, I started praying more, and when I felt the unction, I went to church. My godparents invited me to come to the Church Revival they were having. It was a powerful church service; God was moving in a miraculous way. My godfather had what you call a "Supernatural Deliverance" Ministry.

I remember being in a church service and witnessed what would be one of my first miracles. Godfather stood firmly at the pulpit with his long, black velvet cape that buttoned around his neck, his eyes looked glassy, his right hand held the microphone, and his left hand moved back and forth on his hip. *"Yes, Lord; Yes, Lord; Yes, Lord. I hear You, Lord," he said as he paced* back and forth over the pulpit.

The crowd was praising God by clapping their hands and screaming "Hallelujah," but their eyes were fixed on Pastor Pulley because they knew God was about to do something big that they certainly didn't want to miss. He stepped down the two steps from the pulpit and stood on the altar and said in a stern monotone voice, "I hear God saying that there is a woman in this room, who the doctors just diagnosed with cancer. They have given her six to nine months to live."

Immediately, a high-pitched wailing came from a woman, who was sitting in the back of the crowd, rocking back and forth in a wooden chair. "Come here, my daughter, is that you?" he said as he walked down the center aisle of the church in her direction. Her face was beet red from the tears and emotion of the moment. She got up from her seat and walked to the center aisle. She nodded her head up and down slowly and said, "Yes," while she swung her arms from the overwhelming emotion. "Have you been diagnosed with cancer?" he asked her again for clarity. Then, he put the microphone near her mouth so that the congregation could hear her response. "Yes," she said into the microphone. "When?" he asked. "Three days ago," she responded.

This woman wasn't a member of his church. She was walking by and decided to come into the church and sit in the back. "God is going to heal you, but you have to make a promise to Him. You have to promise that you will live for Him and tell the testimony of how He healed you," he said as he looked directly in her eyes. "I will," she said. "It's better not to make a vow than to make a vow and not keep it," he said. "I will keep my vow," she said with tears flowing down her face and rocking from side-to-side. "Give me some oil," he requested of his armor-bearer.

"Go get the trash cans," he requested from the ushers. The ushers, dressed in all white, including white hats, went running as fast as they could to the back door to grab the first trash can they saw. They ran back to place the trash can on the right side of the woman. Two women ushers stood behind her, both with folded blue throw sheets over their right shoulder. When everyone was in place, my godfather reached out his right hand for his armor-bearer to put oil on it. His eyes were still glassy, and his focus was totally on God and what He was about to do through him.

"Lift your hands," he said to her. She lifted her shaking hands. He put his right hand on her forehead and began to pray forcefully with extreme authority. "Father, I command in the matchless name of Jesus that this woman be made whole. I speak to the enemy to lose his grip! I cause the cancer today to dry up! You cannot have her! By His Stripes, she is healed!

The woman began to scream! She bent forward, holding her stomach. My *godfather grabbed the trash can at the same time as she began to vomit chucks profusely, the size of golf balls, and then she passed out. The ushers put the* blue covers over her as she laid on the church floor.

The following Sunday, she came to church testifying that she went to the doctor, she had an ultrasound, and the doctors didn't see the mass anymore! My Godfather was known to have what they call a *supernatural deliverance ministry*. Once the word was out about how God was using him to heal the sick, people would come from far and near to be in his church services. People were getting healed from diseases, miracles were happening, and the Gift of Prophecy was flowing.

Chapter Twenty-Two

THE GUEST PREACHER, DRESSED IN a royal blue suit, crisp white shirt, no tie, and a long gold chain that stopped near the middle of his chest, walked down from the pulpit, and made eye contact with me. Immediately, my stomach leaped. I knew what was going to come next. I could have recited what he was about to prophesy to me—almost verbatim. I had stopped counting on the twenty-third time of getting the same prophecy from my godparents, and anytime I would be in the presence of a person that held the gift of prophecy.

"Young lady, stand up," he said. I stood up and raised my hands toward heaven. He began to speak, *"I see wealth all around you. God is going to make you wealthy. You will own businesses; your name will be great, and you will help so many people. The number can't be counted, especially women."*

This was my constant prophecy. I finally had to tell God, "I get it." However, later on in life, I understood that the repetition was necessary as faith comes by hearing and hearing again and again. I shook my head in agreement as he spoke. I knew he was a man of God. I had never met him before, and I'm sure he wasn't in any of the other church services that I attended when I had received this same word of prophecy. I agreed, "Amen," and sat down.

He went to walk away and turned around fast, and he said something different—a new prophecy—one I hadn't heard before. He added, *"My God, My God. I see land and houses all around you. Millions in real estate."* This definitely caught my attention. It was as if I was a missing link to the prophecy puzzle. I was told, over and over about the wealth, owning a business, the greatness of my name, and helping countless people. However, until this day, no one had ever told me how God was going to do it.

Real Estate, I thought. *Hmmm...* I began to go into deep thought. As a little girl, as far back as I could remember, I had a strong fascination with real estate. I loved the houses. I would draw with my Crayola crayons big houses with upstairs, downstairs, backyards, garages, nice kitchens, and bathrooms! I remembered at ten years old, my mom must have seen my love for houses because she took me to ride by neighborhoods with nice houses. I immediately had a flashback of a new development of raised ranch houses in West Haven, next to the Veterans Memorial Hospital. Some were completed, and some weren't. She had pulled in a driveway of one that was under construction.

I was so excited. I was more excited looking at this house being developed than I would have ever been at a candy store! I asked, "Mom, can we look inside." The house was only framed out, so it was easy to gain access and look inside. "I don't think we are supposed to, but let's see," she said as she opened the car door. We walked into the back door of the framed house and entered. I was ecstatic. If I knew then, what I know now, about how God reveals our purpose, I would have known real estate was a big part of my future and the prophecy.

The moment I walked into the house as a little girl, I saw the finished product. I was walking through this unfinished house— there was only a plywood frame—yet, I was telling my mom how it would be finished. I showed her where the sink would be hooked up. Where the stove, refrigerator, and the chandelier would go. Where the closet would go and based on the brackets, what kind of closet doors would be installed.

The house plans were rolled up on the floor of what would be the future living room. I rolled out the plans, studied them for about thirty seconds, and began to point out that I was right about what I had just finished showing my mother. I was able to read building plans at ten years old without any formal training. I suddenly awoke from my deep daydream and said out loud, "Yes, real estate makes sense! It will be natural for me."

The following week at work while sorting mail, I come across what appeared to be junk mail from the Human Resource Department. It was a one-page piece of neon yellow paper folded in half with a generic label on it. The mailer was bundled together by rubber bands with the instructions to deliver to all mailboxes. I began doing my job and putting the yellow papers in the mailboxes.

When all of the mailboxes were full, I went to put the extras on the file cabinet next to the mailboxes. As I was about to walk away, a strange curiosity overtook me. I wondered what information was on the yellow paper. Prior to this, I had never looked at the mail, but this paper had piqued my curiosity. Besides, it had a generic label, and it wasn't addressed to any specific person, so I took one from the file cabinet as if I was stealing and opened it on the way out the door. It read:

Yale Homebuyer Program
Informational Session Tomorrow at Noon
Learn about How You Can Qualify for
$10,000 Down Payment Assistance
and $2,000 per Year as a Tax Rebate.
FREE Event to Employees Lunch Will Be Served

My mouth opened, and my jaw dropped my heart beat fast as I stood in the mailroom startled by what I had just read. I couldn't believe the timing of it. "Roberta, are you okay?" one of the faculty members asked as she came to pick up her mail. "Oh, yes, I'm okay," I said as I folded the paper, put it in my pocket, and walked out of the mailroom.

I was making $9.14 an hour. Even though I had a steady income, and I wasn't dependent on a welfare check anymore, I was still struggling. I wanted to move, but couldn't afford the high rents in the neighborhood I desired to live in. This, however, didn't stop me from dreaming. So, I went home after work, and all I did was daydream.

I became so emotionally involved with my daydreaming of owning a home that I could feel the energy in my body. I got chills when I closed my eyes to imagine my son playing outside in safety and not worrying about bullets coming through the window while he slept. My imaginations felt so real to me, and they couldn't be ignored.

The next day, I attended the first-time home buyer's informational session. There was a woman who spoke on obtaining a mortgage for your home and the steps needed to acquire it. During the session, I felt a sense of excitement and nervousness—all at the same time. I wanted to own a home with everything in me, but I had defeating thoughts in the back of my mind.

You're only 21. You're too young to own a home. You only make $9.14 per hour. You're barely above the poverty line. You can't afford to rent an apartment, so you definitely can't afford to buy a home. You should leave now; You don't belong here. Look around you; only older White people are in the room. You stand out like a sore thumb. They know you sort mail. Just be happy with what you have. You don't need a house.

It felt like a tug-of-war in my mind. I finally had enough of self-inflicted mental torture, and I raised my hand to ask a vital question. *"How much money do you have to make to own a home?"* She answered, "It depends on the kind of house you want to purchase. Let's talk after the seminar." "Okay," I said. Suddenly, a mental calmness came over me. After the informational session, I waited to be the last person to speak with her. I didn't want people to overhear my questions. I was so insecure that I still whispered my questions even though, I was the last person in the room, besides the staff who had put the event together.

"How can I help you?" she asked as she looked at me with a big smile. "I want to buy a house, but I don't have any money. I make $9.14 an hour and I have a son. I want better living arrangements for him. Is it possible?" "Anything is possible," she said while still smiling. I cut her off and rattled on with, "I don't know anything about credit. I never had my credit checked. It is probably bad. I don't have enough savings. I don't think I'm ready to buy a house, and I'll just wait for my income tax check, so I can have a down payment money."

I had counted myself out before I had even begun. I gave myself excuses on why what I had imagined wasn't for me. But God had the right person in front of me, who would keep my mindset on track. Her response was, "Why are you so negative about something where you don't know all of the facts yet?" She smiled and continued, "You may not be able to buy a single-family with your income, but you can buy a multi-family house. In fact, this will help you with your financial struggles. Let's do the math. If your mortgage is $1,000, can you pay it?" "No," I responded quickly. "If your mortgage is $1,000 and you have a tenant paying a rent of $900 towards the mortgage, can you afford it?" "Yes," I responded slowly. She was introducing me to a concept that I had never heard about. "Exactly," she said. She continued, "As far as your credit is concerned, let's pull your credit to see what your score is, and if your score is too low, I'll work with you to get it higher, so you can buy." She patted me on my shoulder and said, "By the way, you have a son who needs a house."

She winked her eye as she handed me her business card with an appointment for the following week on the back of it. She said, "I look forward to working with you to become a first-time homebuyer."

Chapter Twenty-Three

I ENJOYED WORKING AT YALE University, and my supervisor was awesome. She continued to teach me the policies and procedures of the company and the department. I was a sponge absorbing every ounce of knowledge she shared with me. I felt fortunate when I overheard colleagues in other departments complaining about their supervisor. In some ways, it felt as if she was the big sister I needed at that particular time.

I met new associates throughout the department as they would come to pick up the mail. Crystalla and I connected immediately. She would be there waiting for the mail for her supervisor, who was the head chairman of the department. Crystalla was always rushing because she was the type of person who was laser-focused on the task set before her. She was a super communicator who wouldn't cut corners. She was effective, efficient, and she was a determined African American employee. Crystalla and I naturally gravitated to each other and quickly became friends.

"Roberta, I'm about to go to Dunkin Donuts after I drop this mail off at my office. Do you want to come?" "Sure," I replied. I took my coat from behind the door, put it on, and met her in the hallway. It took no time before every day at 10:15 a.m. that Crystalla, and I were heading out the door up York Street taking our fifteen-minute Dunkin Donut coffee break. I began to look forward to our short walks. I loved getting fresh air after being inside the building for hours. We would talk about everything under the sun—from what was going on in the department, who was about to get fired, who was going to quit, marriage, and life after Yale.

"Roberta, how do you do it? I don't have a child, and I'm so tired after working all day. I can't imagine how hard it must be for you," Crystalla said out of sheer concern. "I don't have a choice," I responded. "But Working full-time, taking care of your son and now, you've just started going to Quinnipiac University. That's a lot," she said. "I'm focused on my future, my son deserves a better life, and if I don't provide it, who will?" I responded as I opened the door to Dunkin Donuts. I continued, "I want to buy a house, so I'm meeting with the representative from the Home Buying Program to help me." "But Yale makes you stay in certain tracks in New Haven to qualify for the money, and they aren't the best areas," Crystalla said. "I'm aware, but there are some good areas that I wouldn't mind living in. However, I have to get approved first," I responded.

"My Husband and I purchased a home a few years back, and there is nothing like owning your own home." We waited in line for our turn to order. The cashier greeted us with a smile and asked, "May I take your order?" Crystalla and I ordered the same thing at the same time. "Two medium hazelnut coffees, light, and sweet, please." I pulled out my money to pay for our coffees while she did the same. The cashier looked at us as if to say, "I don't care who pays, so I can move the line behind you." I looked at the line behind me and put my money back in my pocket and said, "Thank you".

On the way walking back to the office, I was observing the trucks getting on the highway and the uniqueness of their logos. I took a deep breath and seemingly out of the "blue sky," I said to Crystalla, "I'm going to own a business one day." "Really, what kind?" she said. I shrugged my shoulders and said, "I don't know." We continued walking back to the office while enjoying our hazelnut coffees. It was easy to talk to Crystalla about my dreams. She never once played the role of the "border bully." She never expressed doubt, and she was receptive to my future aspirations—no matter how "far out there," they seemed to be.

The week passed by fast. I was finally sitting in the waiting room to meet with Mr. Carey, the Human Resource Representative, to become pre-qualified for the Home Buying Program. I was very nervous. I had uncontrollable butterflies in my stomach. Negative thoughts continued to keep going through my mind. *Stop wasting your time. They are going to laugh at you. You're too young. You don't make enough money. You need to be satisfied with what you have. Leave now, they won't notice.*

Although I was nervous, I had my mind made up. I wasn't going to tell myself, "No." I wasn't going to count myself out before I had begun. So, I began to counteract the negative thoughts in my head. Now, I had positive thoughts crossing my mind. *I can do all things through Christ that strengthens me. I am the head and not the tale. I am above and not beneath. If God is for me, who can be against me? I am destined for greatness.*

My mental "tug-of-war" was interrupted by a frail Irish woman with short black hair, who stood five feet tall. "Mr. Carney is ready to meet with you, now," she said. I took a deep breath and cautiously breathed in and then breathed out. "Okay, I'll follow you," I said as I rose from the seat in the waiting area. She took me through what seemed to be a maze. I passed cubicles, offices, coffee stations, and other people passing in the hallway before we finally reached his office.

When I walked in, he stood, shook my hand, and said, "So, you want to buy a house." He had a pleasant smile on his face. "Yes, I do, if I can," I replied, also with a smile. "I looked in the system, and according to my system, you are qualified for the home buyer benefits with up to $10,000 to use towards your down payment and closing costs. You will receive $2,000 per year as tax reimbursements for up to ten years. You must stay in the house for five years and remain employed at Yale University. If you discontinue employment at Yale, your tax reimbursement will discontinue. The $10,000 will be given to you as a forgivable loan. The loan will be forgivable at a rate of 20 percent per year, so if you stay in the home for five years, you don't have to pay anything back. However, if you move before the five years is up, you will be responsible for paying back the loan balance that hasn't been forgiven. All you have to do is sign on the dotted line that you agree and your all set with me," he explained.

Shocked and still nervous, I signed the agreement letter as fast as I could that he had already printed and had waiting for me. He gave me a carbon copy and said, "Congratulations, now, carry this paperwork to Arleen, and she will take it from there." I nearly ran out of the office! When I got outside, I jumped up and down, screaming emotionally and punching the air with excitement. "Thank you, Jesus, Thank you, Jesus, Thank you, Jesus, I knew it!"

This was the first time that I had recalled being intentional about winning the battle of my mindset. The prophecy that was given to me, gave me the added faith when fear was trying to make me retreat from my big blessing.

Can you imagine how my life would have been if I had allowed fear to conquer my faith?

At this point in my life, I felt free. I knew I was on the right track and that God had just opened the door for me. All I had to do was to continue winning the battle of my mind and begin listening to my inner spirit. I knew I was on to something, and it was the beginning of something great. But I had no idea, how great!

Shortly, after learning about being pre-approved, I found out that I was pregnant with my second child. So, here I was, once again, juggling life, being a single mom, working a full-time job, going to school in the evening, looking for a house, being a girlfriend, and now, pregnant with my second child.

I had so many mixed emotions going through my mind. One was that I didn't want to be the girl with a bunch of different baby daddies. If I was going to have another child, I needed to be married. I was in a strong relationship at the time, and marriage made sense.

The next few months consisted of meetings with Arlene and my real estate agent. Arlene was an old school Italian lady, who didn't allow for any excuses. I felt like I saw 100 houses before I found the four-family house, which made financial sense for my situation.

I wrote it down: Potential Rent of 283 Norton Street, New Haven, CT.

- Unit 1(2 bedrooms): $900
- Unit 1A (2 room): $600
- Unit 2 (3 bedrooms): My Apartment (Rent Free)
- Unit 3 (3 bedrooms): $1,100

- Monthly Income: $2,600
- Monthly Mortgage: $1,100

Monthly Cash Flow: $1,500 (After the mortgage was paid).

This property just made financial sense. I moved forward with the process to acquire the property, but not without challenges. If it wasn't one thing, it was another. I kept on fighting for my home as I knew that anything worth having is worth fighting for, so along with Arlene, I fought.

We finally got the final approval to close on the home, and the biggest obstacle showed up—I went into labor. "Arlene, I'm about to give birth, I can't close," I said to her on her voicemail, and I hung up the phone. "I need pain medicine," I said to the doctors as I laid on the hospital bed. "Please, give me pain medicine, NOW!" "Hold on, Miss. Hoskie, we're preparing it, now."

Suddenly, the contractions started coming more frequently. "WHOOOOOOOOOOOOOOOOOOOA. WHOOO OOOOOOOOOOOOA," I screamed as I held on to the bars of the bed. "Miss. Hoskie, we are going to need you to calm down. Please, sit on the side of the bed, arch your back, and take a deep breath in and out before we can administer the epidural," the nurse said.

It took everything in me to cooperate. I remember that I wasn't able to be given pain medicine with my first child, and I surely didn't want to repeat the same level of pain. The anesthesiologist put a brown clipboard with a waiver form that had required my signature. They wanted me to sign that I wouldn't sue the hospital if anything went wrong during the procedure. I didn't think twice, I signed and shortly, after that I received my medicine. I was calm. Perhaps, too calm. I didn't have the energy to push. I was too calm. This alarmed the doctors.

"If you don't push, your baby will not make it. Push, Push, NOW!" the doctor screamed to spark my attention. I pushed with all I had, and on January 27th, God blessed me with a baby boy, My Oliver.

Next, I had an allergic reaction to the anesthesia. My entire body was itching. It felt like I had 100 little bugs taking turns biting me while being nervous and drowsy at the same time. When the hospital phone rang, I nearly jumped out of my skin.

"Hello," I said. "Congratulations! What did you have?" "A boy. Who is this?" I said. "It's Arlenea. I got your message about not being able to close, but girl you must be crazy because I'm on my way to the hospital for you to sign the proxy paperwork, so you can have a house to go home to," she said. "Are you serious? You're coming to the hospital?" I replied. "You're absolutely right. I'll be there in fifteen minutes." And she did. Arlene was at the hospital in fifteen minutes with the paperwork for me to sign. Some people thought she was too bold, but she was just what I needed! I closed on my first home at 283 Norton Street in New Haven, CT.

Chapter Twenty-Four

I QUICKLY ADJUSTED TO BECOMING a mom again. My department gave me the biggest and best baby shower a person could ever imagine! Oliver had everything from savings bonds to furniture and diapers for an entire year! We didn't unpack his belongings; we just piled it in the moving truck to be brought to my new home. Shortly after, I was married with children. Life was good and back to normal.

A few months later, I was awakened from a deep sleep. "Oh, my God," I said as I went running to the bathroom as fast as I could. "Bluth." Vomit was all over the pink walls and the floors. I continued to vomit throughout the entire day. There was a stomach bug going around, but I wanted to be sure I wasn't pregnant again. So, the next morning, I went to Walgreens and purchased a pregnancy test.

Oliver was just learning how to walk. He crawled fast and would follow me everywhere I went. "Wait right here, Snoota" I said in a calm, polite way as I went to the bathroom to take the pregnancy test. Snoota was Oliver's nickname. My heart was beating fast, and my palms were profusely sweating as I waited for the results. I put the test on the vanity and waited. One Stripe…two stripes! Whoa! I screamed, put my hands on my head, swung the bathroom door open, and ran to my bedroom. I laid across the bed and put my head on the pillow. I was in total shock. I had just started getting my life back on track with school, work, being a wife, and mother of two small children. *Oliver was still in diapers and wasn't fully walking, yet and another child Was on its way,* I thought.

Before the shock could settle, Oliver pushed my door open with the pregnancy test in his hand and said, "Hun" his way of saying "here" as he handed me the pregnancy test with wide innocent glossy eyes. He clearly thought he was helping his mother by returning what he thought I had lost in the bathroom. He stood, looking at me, waiting for my response to see if my expression would change. He wanted me to smile. So, I did. I smiled, gave him a big hug and kiss, and then said: "Thank you, Honey." He smiled from ear-to-ear and crawled away.

My husband was happy as I showed him the test. He hugged me and said, "At least your married". Yes, I was married. The thought of being a single mother statistic didn't haunt me anymore.

When Diege found out that he had another brother or sister on the way, he immediately responded innocently, "Isn't this too soon; we just had one?" He must have heard someone say this, so he was just repeating it.

My pregnancy was very hard. Five months into my pregnancy, my husband had an altercation in the barbershop where he was working. The man he fought, decided not to have a fair fight, and shot him, making him unable to walk or to care for himself. He began losing weight and becoming angry. Not only was he in a vulnerable state, but he also had no money coming into the home to contribute to the family.

This made life very stressful, I was five months pregnant, working full-time, going to school, taking care of two young children, and taking care of a semi-paralyzed husband, who has also become verbally abusive.

Nine months later, I gave birth to my baby girl, Allia. The doctors said that I was having a boy, but God surprised us all with a precious little girl. The delivery didn't go without complication. I had to stop pushing during labor because the umbilical cord was wrapped around her neck. When she was born, she wasn't breathing, and she was a bluish-greenish color. My mother was in the hospital, praying and binding the devil. She saw what I didn't see. She saw the doctors under a controlled panic, and that my baby girl wasn't breathing.

"What's going on? …Why isn't my baby crying?" I said hysterically, as I attempted to sit up, but was restrained by being connected to the monitors. My body suddenly became tense and stiff as a board on the delivery table. "What's going on?" I kept repeating my question with no answers. Then, abruptly. I heard her weak little cry. My body immediately relaxed. I laid my head to the side, closed my eyes, and said, "Thank you, Jesus!"

Now, I was a mom of three, and it seemed to have happened overnight. Dante was my little helper. I had two babies, both in diapers with two bags to pack and double everything—double stroller, double dressing, and double crying. It was almost as if I was raising twins. It was hard, learning to manage life's everyday duties—again.

Although I was married, I was often alone. I battled depression while I fought to keep my family together. However, after a while, my marriage came to a tragic, violent end, and *I became a single mother again, but this time with three children.*

*****

My dedication and hard work at Yale had paid off. I was promoted four times in the same department and was now the Assistant Administrator for the entire department. I loved the position. One day, I was asked to come upstairs for a quick meeting. I thought it was about the departmental finances, but I was offered a job that I couldn't refuse. One of the Division Chairmen at Yale accepted a position as the Chairman at Albert Einstein College of Medicine and asked if I would accompany him as the Department Administrator for Research. He doubled my salary. I had a six-figure salary and a chauffeur that would bring me home when I worked late (the job was in New York City). Many people thought I had made it and I did too! My grandmother was so proud. She would often say, "My granddaughter works with them, rich doctors." And it made me feel good. Life was good.

My real estate investment had been good to me. When I needed to stay home from work and take extended time off, my bills were paid because of my real estate investment. The mortgage was being paid by my third-floor tenant, who had Section 8 (the Housing Voucher Program). I lived rent and mortgage free, and the other two units provided cash flow of $1500 per month. For the first time in my life, I was able to breathe financially.

Although I purchased a multi-family property, I had no idea of the "power of real estate," or shall I say, "the power of equity." "How much equity do you have in your house?" It was a question that was posed by a total stranger. "What's equity?" I responded. I had no idea what equity was. In fact, I had never even heard of the word before. So, of course, I didn't know how much equity was in my property because I didn't know what equity was.

However, I later found out that equity is the difference between the debt service of the property and the property's appraised value. I was told that equity was why people purchased houses, and it was an equivalent to having money in the bank. Well, I didn't purchase my house for equity. I purchased it because I was trying to survive, but I was certainly curious to see how much "money in the bank" I had accumulated.

To my surprise, my property appraised at $300,000! I purchased it for 88,000. According to the equation, my house had $220,000 in equity! This was mind-blowing to me. I hadn't done anything to the property to increase the value of it. I just lived there and maintained it. I put the property on the market, and within thirty days, I had a full price offer! My brain cells were definitely working. I thought that I just hit the Lotto!

But I didn't want to be like the person who hit the lotto one day and the next day was poor again. I realized that this was the chance of a lifetime, and I had to be strategic. I put the money in my bank account, and it sat there until I had a plan. I wouldn't spend one penny of it—I was scared to. I had never seen this much money before. I went to the bank two or three times a day just to get a balance print out to be sure the money was still in the account. It was still there waiting for a plan. So, I prayed, prayed, and prayed. I sat at my kitchen table, pulled out a piece of paper and a pen to calculate how much money this property had produced for me, and all I could do was shake my head in amazement.

283 Norton Street

- $109, 200 = Rental Income
- $9, 800 = Garage Income
- $6,000 = Tax Rebates
- $212,000 = Gross Proceeds from Sale
- $337,000 = Total Income

Wow! This one property had given me over a quarter of a million dollars, and I made the money unintentionally.

Chapter Twenty-Five

THE AWAKENING

I THOUGHT, AND I WONDERED... *What would happen if I did it intentionally?*

Then, I was bitten by the real estate bug. I started flipping properties. I took the cash I had in the bank and purchased a single-family house in the Westville area of New Haven for $100,000. I put $25,000 in repairs and within ninety days sold it for $299,900. The next property, I purchased from the Government for 30,000. I put $40,000 in repairs, and within sixty days after completion, I sold the property for $210,000.

It was as if God was preparing me for this day. I already knew all of the comparable properties in the area because every day of the work week for the prior two years, I studied the real estate market on my commute to work. Every day I would do the same thing, on my way running for the 7:27 a.m. train, I would grab every real estate magazine in the train station and study it on the commute. I was able to tell you what houses sold, which houses were on the market, how long they were on the market, and if the prices had to be reduced to sell it. As I previously said, I just loved real estate. I thought I was amusing myself by looking at the magazines, but God was preparing me for greater times.

I continued to acquire, rehab, and sell properties. I was making more than my annual salary—close to every ninety days! Word spread fast that I was a Real Estate Investor. Soon, people would call me to purchase their houses from them because they were going through personal problems, such as divorce. Also, I received many requests for me to help because the owner was "upside down." Upside down in real estate terms means that you owe more on the property, then the actual value of the property. In other words, the property has negative equity.

This became a common scenario as the onset of the Housing Market Crisis began to set in. Many people didn't know what to do with their properties as interest rates adjusted and balloon payments become due. The real estate industry was very relaxed at the time. The mortgage brokers were giving away "stated loans". This is the type of loan where you wouldn't need proof of income; you could be approved based on what you "stated" as income on the mortgage application. This mortgage product, along with the interest-only— mortgage product was popular during this time period.

Many people were getting approved for mortgages that they simply couldn't afford. I'm sure people stated whatever income they needed to state to make the mortgage go through. The interest-only mortgage product was also a popular one. It, too, approved people for mortgages they couldn't afford. With the interest-only mortgage product, the borrower would pay only the interest on the mortgage note for the first two years and then the mortgage payment would increase substantially when the principal became due. The thought process at the time was immediate gratification. You can get what you want now, and in two years, you can refinance and get into a better mortgage product. However, many people didn't know that in two years, it would become virtually impossible to get a loan, and refinancing was out of the question. The housing market crash was a sad time for many people, but was a "gold mine" for the savvy investor, like myself.

Warren Buffett had given advice years prior, and it stuck with me. He said, "When the Government tells you not to buy, you buy. And when they tell you to buy, you don't." During this time, the media declared a housing crisis and urged people not to buy homes. People were so consumed by the negative media of the housing market that they were afraid to buy. But this was just the opportunity I needed.

The good old law of "supply and demand" was in full effect. The supply of housing was increasing, and the demand was decreasing, which caused the prices of homes to decline. I was in the perfect position. I do not believe in coincidence; I believe God has his hand in it all.

When I *happened* to purchase my first property right before the housing market increased and when I *happened* to cash out right before the market crashed. This put me in the best financial position since I had the cash to invest while others couldn't get a mortgage.

Real estate was natural to me, and I loved it! I continued to work, but the commute to and from New York was becoming stressful. It was taking too much time away from my family. One day, I came home from work, and my daughter was walking. This broke my heart. I missed her first steps. I knew it was time for a change. I applied for countless jobs, did telephone interviews, and nothing happened to bring about a change. I was so unsettled, and I wanted to change, but I felt like I should be satisfied with how far I had come. After all, I was no longer on welfare, I was making six figures, and I had a Chauffer.

I was crying on my ride to work because I felt like I was a *bad* person. I felt like I was a greedy person, and my mother had told me not to be greedy when I was growing up. So, I began to cry and pray.

Father, forgive me for not being satisfied. I feel like there is more and I want it. But I don't want to be a greedy person. My mother taught me to 'be satisfied,' but I don't know how. I thank You for my good-paying job. You have brought me a mighty long way from being on welfare, and I thank You. I'm sorry, but please help me to be satisfied. I want to please you. Father, please help me. Why am I this way?

As soon as I had asked, "Why am I this way?" after complete silence, God *spoke to me, "Because I made you that way."* Immediately a calm peace came over me. It made sense. I didn't give myself an inner drive. So, I asked another question, "Why did you make me this way?" God spoke again, *"Because you have much work to do, so you can't be satisfied. I am a big God, and the entire world belongs to me… never settle."*

The next day when I was running to catch the 7:27 a.m. train, as usual, I grabbed all of the real estate magazines on the way to the train. I started flipping through the magazines and checking on what properties had been sold, what properties were on the market, and what properties were recently reduced.

While simultaneously asking God, "Please show me my next move, Father." Then, I would turn the page of the real estate magazine and continue talking to God. *"I know You have something for me, please, reveal it God,"* I said as *I* picked up the next real estate magazine. *"It seems like doors just aren't opening up, God. What shall I do?" I asked* as I continued to look at the real estate magazines. I took a deep breath since I was beginning to feel defeated. I threw the real estate magazine on the seat next to me. I put my face in my hands, closed my eyes, and said, *"God, please, reveal to me what's next. Amen."*

My day continued as normal. I clocked into the office, checked my email, voicemails, and made my "to do" list for the day. While I was in the office, I was focused. Often, I would be so focused on the project I was working on that I would forget about lunch or a break. I would work straight through until it was time to catch the train back to CT.

However, this day was a little different, as I decided to take a walk outside to get some fresh air and to purchase lunch from the outside vendors, who sold food from their vans, or shall I say, their kitchen on wheels. While I waited in line, I sparked a conversation with a gentleman by the name of Damien, whom I would often see in passing. He worked for a Financial Company that purchased and sold non-performing mortgage notes. When we would see each other, it would always spark a good conversation. However, this day for some reason, he wasn't himself. He looked very stressed.

"Hey, Damien, how are you? Are you okay?" I asked. "Yes, I'm good," he said in his Jamaican accent. He continued, "I'm just tired of this project I'm doing in Connecticut. My company decided to buy and hold the property, instead of selling it. So, I'm in charge of renovating it, and we are behind schedule and losing money." "Where is the property in Connecticut?" I responded. "New Haven," he said. "New Haven?" I asked in shock. "Yes, on Cedar Hill," he said. "Damien, do you know I'm from New Haven, and I commute to the Bronx, every day," I said excitedly. "Really, I didn't know that," he said. "Listen, I can help you. I'm in New Haven every day. I renovate and flip properties. I definitely know how to manage teams," I cheerfully responded. "Wow, I'm going to take you up on your offer," he said and pulled out a pen and paper to write my phone number down. "Absolutely, it would be my pleasure," I said with a broad smile. We exchanged numbers, and I ordered my lunch from the van—jerk chicken and cabbage.

The next day, Damien called me, asking if I was able to meet him at the property on Saturday since he would be in New Haven. He had wanted to show me the property, what had been done, and what needed to be done in order for the project to be complete.

The property was 95 percent completed and looked beautiful. It was a six-family unit—each unit had three bedrooms with open layouts, new kitchens, new baths, new mechanicals, and even laundry was available. "We're losing so much money on this house. The repairs are way over budget. It seemed like when we thought we had fixed one thing, then another thing needs to be fixed," Damien explained as he pointed out the things that were unfinished. "Why don't you start the rental process to get some money coming in?" I said. "They aren't finished," he said. "Just get me a model unit, finish this apartment, and I'll rent the building out for you," I said. "I didn't think of that, but it's a good idea."

He called the contractors, who were working throughout the building and told them to all focus on completing unit-1L, today. The model was complete and ready for me the next day. I was very happy to help him. The next week, I ran advertisements, held an open house, and rented all six units at $1,100 per unit, giving him a rent roll of $6,600 per month in one day! "Thank you so much, Roberta," he said with great relief. "You're very welcome, and it was fun," I said as I got into my car leaving the property.

I felt such a sense of accomplishment. I was so happy to see the smile on his face. The following week, Damien called me at work, asking me to come downstairs to meet him outside of the building. I thought there was an emergency, so I immediately left my office, took the elevator to the ground floor, and went outside. Damien was standing there on his phone. When he saw me, he motioned for me to wait one minute. When he finished his call, he handed me an envelope with a check for $2,500 and said: "I could have never done it without you." Then the mental "light bulb" came on. You mean to tell me, I can get paid for something I would have done for free! I thanked Damien, put the check in my pocketbook, and went back into my office.

It was a long demanding day at work. We were working on a grant to bring in over ten million in research dollars. I was the administrator in charge of coordinating the program project grant with five other faculty members and their staff. The deadline was approaching, so the stress in the office was high. If the grant wasn't approved, eight faculty members and researchers working in my boss's lab would lose the funding for their salary. If this were to happen, it would be catastrophic to the research my boss had performed for over the past twenty years.

He published national and international articles on his research on the Effects of Hypoxia using Drosophila as the test sample. We needed the funding to continue his research and to keep his research team intact. It was very stressful. I worked in the office until 2 a.m. to meet the submission deadline. "It's 2 a.m. How do you still run around as if it's 2 p.m.," I asked my Boss, who always had a lot of energy. "I run every day at 5 a.m., but my life work is on the line. I have people and their life depending on me. I can't get sleep," he responded.

I nodded my head in agreement, as I continued rushing to put the 500-page grant in order to put it into the FedEx box. "Did you call, your driver to be sure he's downstairs to take you home?" he asked. "Yes, he called about ten minutes ago letting me know that he is downstairs waiting on me," I responded. "We're done as soon as you seal the box," he said. "Box sealed, and I'm going home to my family," I said as I handed him the taped FedEx box. I stood up, started packing my belongings in my briefcase, grabbed my pocketbook from under the desk, and headed downstairs to my chauffeur, who had been waiting patiently to take me home.

"Hello, Ms. Roberta, I take it you had a long day at the office," Mike, my driver, said as he opened the door for me to get into the back seat of his black Lincoln Town Car. "Yes, Mike, it was," I responded as I put my briefcase in the car and sat down. I took a deep breath, dropped my head to the back of the headrest, and exhaled. "I hope you found some good in today, Ms. Roberta," Mike said as he looked at me through his rear-view mirror. "In fact, I did," I said as I opened my pocketbook and pulled out the check Damien had given me. I continued, "I got paid for something I would have done for free." "Whatcha talkin' bout, Ms. Roberta," he said with a smile on his face glancing at the rear-view mirror. "I helped a colleague out with a real estate development project that he has in New Haven, and he gave me this check to thank me," I explained as I looked at the check.

"If you don't mind me asking, how much did he give you?" "Two Thousand Five Hundred Dollars," I responded. "Oh, that's no little money. I thought you were going to say Two Hundred and Fifty, not Two Thousand and Five hundred," he said. "Yeah, I had fun helping him with his property because something felt really natural about it," I said as I put the check back in my pocketbook and pulled out the real estate magazines that I had collected from the train station on my way going into the office.

Once again, I opened the magazine, turned the pages, looked at all of the houses for sale, which properties sold, and which properties were reduced. I took a deep breath and closed my eyes and silently prayed. *God, what is my next move. I can't keep doing these late nights. My family needs me. Father, please, show me my next move. Amen.*

I opened my eyes, picked up the next real estate magazine, and God said in a soft tone, "Your looking at it." My mouth dropped open. My eyes got big, and I could feel butterflies in my stomach, and I said, *"Real Estate!"*

Chapter Twenty-Six

LEAVING THE PLANTATION

Dear Dr. H.,

Thank you so much for the opportunity to work beside you for the past two years. I have learned so much from you in such a short period of time. I also learned a lot about myself. When I first accepted this job, I didn't know what to expect. To be honest, I thought, I was in over my head when I showed up for the first day of work to no phones, no furniture, no staff, no office policies, and no office procedures. However, I'm happy that I stayed and took on the challenge to establish the department from nothing to what it is today. In just two years, we created a sustainable department, brought in over $20,000,000 in grants, and contracts, and furthered your research. We maintained and created jobs. I truly believe that all of this was great preparation for the new steps that I will be taking in my life. I have decided to pursue real estate full-time,

*and I will be starting a property management com-
pany. You have shown me through your research that
in life, it's important to pursue your life purpose and
passion; and this is what I will be doing during this
next chapter in my life.*

*Please accept this letter as my thirty notice of
my intent to terminate my employment at Albert
Einstein College of Medicine. Again, thank you for
the wonderful opportunity.*

*Sincerely,
Roberta*

AFTER DR. H. FINISHED READING the letter, he sat back in his plush brown leather seat, looked at me and said, "What are your plans after here?" "I'm going to do real estate full-time," I responded. "Real estate? Ha! Good luck!" he said in a sarcastic tone and turned around in his seat to continue his work.

This certainly wasn't the response I thought I would receive from him. Nevertheless, I wasted no time with coordinating my next steps. God had spoken, and I was crystal clear about the direction of my life. It was time to put an end to working late nights, and the four-hour commute back and forth from Connecticut to New York. I needed to be home with my family. My children were growing up, and I was missing it. I'll never forget the day I came home after working late to see my daughter walking around. My heart broke to pieces because I was too busy with my job that I missed her first steps. That was the trigger to begin the search for a new direction.

So, yes, I resigned from my six-figure job to follow my heart and started my business in my basement, along with my Sister, Tameka. She was my God-given mastermind partner. She was 100 percent on board and believed in the vision, and God knew I needed her.

Many people thought I had lost my mind and sometimes, I did too for leaving a six-figure job with a chauffeur, especially when you're in your twenties. At that time, it was crazy and unheard of to chase something invisible! Yes, my Divinely Revealed Event Awaiting

Manifestation (DREAM) of being an entrepreneur was invisible to the outside world, but inside, I saw it clearly! I knew that God was calling me higher. There was an urgency in my spirit that I couldn't explain. My drastic decision wasn't about money; it was about freedom and fulfilling "divine destiny".

I believed this was the direction that God was calling me to make a difference in the world. From the outside, I looked like an insane fool, but from the inside, I knew God would use me to His Glory through my business, and He would be sure that I got the last laugh. So, I put on blinders to people and their opinions of me while I conquered my fears, looked inside of myself to see my future, and trusted that God would bring me through the process. After all, I knew I wasn't starting just an ordinary real estate company; I was starting a Ministry of Helps. It was going to be a company with an outreach to the community.

Therefore, it was only fitting that the name of the company be entitled Outreach. But even more fitting because the name of my godparent's church was Outreach for Christ, and I felt that my business was an extension of their ministry. I learned in business that the name says it "all," or it says nothing. So, yes, Outreach, said it all to me.

To keep start-up cost low, I used what I had. Outreach's first office was my leaking basement, and it didn't matter. My sister and I were focused. We had an old school, black, single-line phone that we purchased for $9.99 and a fax machine. The phone had two distinct rings, one which would alert us that we had a business call coming in and another distinct ring that would alert us to run fast to connect the fax machine. Our total start-up cost was less than $200. We were in business!

The first month of working from home, felt like I was playing hooky from work and that I was doing something wrong. I had to ask my attorney if it was legal for me to sign my own paycheck. It felt so unnatural and illegal. The check was $1,000 payable to "Roberta Hoskie" signed by "Roberta Hoskie" and endorsed by "Roberta Hoskie." How could this be?

You can't sign your own paycheck, I thought. But my attorney assured me that I was a business owner now, not an employee, and business owners sign their own paychecks! It was a new concept that I didn't adapt to easily.

Outreach definitely had growing pains, since the real estate market had crashed, and my real estate investing money sources came to a complete halt. There were times when I thought I had made a huge mistake.

My sister and I would keep the faith and keep good spirits even though we had no money in the account and no idea how money was going to come in. It had gotten to the point that we were happy when we would receive the $30 application fee because this meant we had lunch money. God definitely assigned my sister to help keep the business alive with faith when mine got a little weak. However, together, we stayed focused.

The Company began to grow. We purchased a little black fragile metal desk; it was in the kitchen up against the wall as you first walked in. My kitchen and my kitchen walls were my way of transforming the area into a workspace. I scotch taped my business projections, business plans, to do list and quick references, all over the kitchen wall above my black metal desk.

After about a year of working from home, God opened up a door for us to move into our first "real" office. As usual, my sister and I were walking by faith when we saw the for-rent sign in the window. I inquired and set up a showing of the storefront on 588 East Street, New Haven, CT. The owner met us at the space and showed us around. It was just what we needed, but it was out of our budget at $900 per month. After showing us the space, the owner asked what we thought of the place. I immediately responded, "I love it, and it's perfect for us, but unfortunately, we can't afford it." "Can you afford $875 per month?" he said. "That's steep for us, we are just starting," I responded. "Can you afford $800 per month? he asked this time. My sister and I looked at each other because, at that point, we knew God was moving.

"That's still steep," I responded. "Okay," he said. The owner started turning off the lights and heading towards the door to see us out. Then he stopped and said, "I'll tell you what, my wife and I own multiple buildings, and we travel often. Maybe we can barter. If you can be our property management company when we travel, I will give you the space for $600." My Sister and I looked at each other and smiled. And I said, "Done deal." We were so happy about leaving our new office space. We didn't immediately leave because we praised God in the car, then laughing and shaking our heads. Yes, once again, walking by faith had paid off.

Having a real office allowed us to grow, and we no longer had to meet clients at the nearest coffee shop to handle business, and it felt good for a change. Eventually, we asked our brother, Emanuel, to come to the rescue, since we needed a good salesperson. Neither my sister, nor I had sales experience, but he did, and he was good at it. Bringing Manny on, infused a new life, new energy, and some of his money within the company to keep us all a float.

Becoming an entrepreneur definitely had its pros and cons. No two days were ever the same, especially during the time we had no income, which certainly proved to be the most challenging. Some days, I felt like retreating, closing down the business and going to get my job back at Yale. These were the times I prayed the hardest and reminded myself of the prophecies that were spoken over my life.

It was hard. My son was enrolled in a private school, and when the income stopped flowing, I didn't know how I was going to pay for his tuition. I went to the mailbox to get the mail. There was a green and white envelope with my son's school in the top left corner. I took a deep breath, went inside my house, proceeded upstairs to my bedroom with the envelope in my hand. My children must have felt something was wrong.

"You okay, Mom?" Oliver said, and Dante and Allia starred in concern. "Yes, honey, I'm fine," I responded as I quickly ran up the stairs. "You don't look fine," Dante said. "I'm Good, honey. I'm fine, love you," I yelled from the top of the stairs. I went into the room, lifted the envelope up to God, and prayed an emotionally heartfelt prayer.

Father, Lord in the name of Jesus, I thank You for everything You have done in my life. I thank You for loving me when I didn't love myself. I thank

*you because Your word is true. You are not a man
that You shall lie. You are the truth, the way, and
the light. You are the Alpha and the Omega, the
Beginning, and the End. You are mighty and have
all the power in Your hands, and I worship You.*

*Now, Father, You are greater than the bill col-
lectors and certainly greater than my baby's school.
Father, You know what I have need of before I ask.
But Father, I ask for Your wisdom and favor. I know
that in this envelope is a bill for over $13,000 that
I do not have right now. I also, know that they are
threatening not to allow my baby to graduate and
Father, we can't have this. You opened this door for
my baby to go there and You will not allow any man
to shut it. He is 'destined for greatness.' Father, You
gave me my children, and I gave each and every one
of them back to You for Your service and for Your
glory. Lord, I need You to grant Your favor, and I
thank You in advance, so my son will graduate! He
will walk across the stage. He will graduate, and
no mortal man will stand in his way! Now, Father,
go with me as I go to this school. I know You have
already made the way. Amen.*

I grabbed my pocketbook, the keys to my car off of my dresser,
kissed my children on the forehead, and said, "Mommy, will be
back." I played gospel music the entire ride to his school. I parked
and went into what appeared to be a little cape single-family home.
This building was the Bursar's Office. I went into the office with all
of my faith to have a conversation and to come to an agreement. I
made up my mind that I wasn't leaving without a solution because
my son was going to graduate.

"Hello, my name is Roberta, and I'm Dante's mother. I need to
speak with someone about my bill." I said as I stood in the front recep-
tion area. "Yes, Ms. Hoskie, please have a seat, someone will be with
you in a minute," the woman with a short bob hair cut responded.

Before I could sit down, a lady came from the back and said, "Hello, can help you," and she opened the door, allowing me to come to the back of the office. "Thank you for seeing me today. I owe a balance, and I need to make payment arrangements." I explained as I handed her the letter that had come in the mail earlier. "Okay, Ma'am. Let me see what I can do for you," she responded as she left the conference room that we were sitting in.

I closed my eyes, and underneath my breath, I began to praise God in advance as I knew she was going to speak to someone who was able to make a decision about the arrangement for my bill and allow my son to graduate. "Lord, I thank You because You already worked it out. Hallelujah, Hallelujah, Hallelujah, Hallelujah!"

She returned with another woman, and they sat at the conference room table. "Hello, Ms. Hoskie, I'm the Assistant Bursar. I was told that you want to make a payment arrangement on your bill," she said. "Yes, I do," I responded. "Our policy doesn't allow for graduation unless the bill is paid in full. Graduation is six weeks away. Will you have it paid by then?" "I don't think I will be able to pay it in full in six weeks. I am a real estate agent. I have a few closings coming up in the next two weeks. I can give you $8,000 when they close," I said. "That's good, but our policy won't allow for your child to graduate with an outstanding bill," she responded.

There was an awkward silence. I'm sure she expected me to say, "Okay and leave." But I wasn't leaving until we came to an agreement and my son was graduating. I believed that God would show up and show favor. So, I was trusting Him at his word. "Well, Ms. Hoskie, what's your child's name?" she asked. "Dante Brito," I responded. "Oh, Dante. We love him. He is such a great kid!" The energy in the meeting immediately changed. "Well, I know what the policy is, but if you come up with $8,000 in the next two weeks, I will sign-off allowing him to graduate, and we will work out an agreement on the balance."

My stiff body turned limp, and my head hung. I inhaled and exhaled and held my head back up. I stood up to shake their hands and with tears in my eyes, said, "Thank you both, so much. God Bless you."

I could have run to the car because I was overwhelmed with happiness. God showed up! It was as if a fifty-pound weight had been removed from my shoulders! As much as I wanted to dance outside the Bursar's Office, I kept my composure until I got back into my car. I let out the loudest "Hallelujah!" with all of my might and energy. God had just won the battle for me!

It was hard going from making six figures every sixty to ninety days to basically, having no income due to the real estate market crash and trying to grow my business. However, God had supplied all of my needs, according to the power that worked within me and according to my faith.

Chapter Twenty-Seven

CRAZY FAITH

IT WAS THE RELENTLESS "CRAZY faith" that propelled me back into prosperity over the next few years. God gave me back everything I had lost and much more. He rewarded my faithfulness and prospered my business in the middle of what the Government called the recession. I was actually in the best position any real estate company could have been in because we focused on property management and tenant placement, not just property sales.

When the recession hit, people weren't able to purchase or sell properties. The only options left was to hire property managers to keep their properties afloat and to rent the properties. So, we were poised for success in the midst of the real estate storm.

I continued to study Real Estate Investing Techniques and learned real estate and business marketing strategies. Every day I would listen to audiobooks, such as Think and Grow Rich by Napoleon Hill. I also forced my children to listen to the audiobooks too to start transforming their mindset with the things I was just learning about like, the Law of Attraction from the book The Secret by Rhonda Byrne.

I was taught in church to "think on those things that are good" and "as a man thinketh, so is he," but the way it was being explained in the audiobooks made it much more plain and simpler to under-stand and to apply to my life.

I was so focused on learning that I did something I had never done before. I attended my first formal Real Estate Brokers Training. This was a training for all of the business owners of Real Estate Brokerages. I was happy to attend and learn more, but the moment I walked into the hotel and stood in the line for registration, I imme-diately noticed something strange.

It looked like all 200 attendees were in uniform and I clearly didn't get the memo stating, "The business owners of Real Estate Brokerages must wear black or blue suits with crisp white shirts, and either a red, blue, or yellow tie." I also didn't get the memo stating this was an older "White men only training."

I pulled out my phone and looked at my confirmation of regis-tration. I was in the right place, but clearly "out of place." This was my rude awakening that the "high level" real estate industry is dom-inated by older White men. I clearly didn't fit their typical mold; in fact, I shattered it, when I walked in the room! I was a Black, young female, and I was wearing a hot pink knee-length dress with sexy silver stilettos. All of the black and blue suited White men laughed, exchanged business cards, and talked about how well their company was doing.

Feeling awkward was an understatement. I sat alone to the far left of the room in the row of seats lining the wall. Only one per-son greeted me as I sat and waited for the training to begin. "Hello, my name is Bill. How are you doing?" he asked as he extended his hand out for a handshake. "Hello, Bill. My name is Roberta, and I'm doing well," I said in my most proper voice. "Who are you here with today?" he asked. "No one," I responded. "Oh, what company are your representing today?" he asked. "Outreach Realty," I casually responded. "Outreach Realty, I've heard of the company. I know the broker. He's a cool guy and knows his stuff about this real estate industry," he confidently said to me. I smiled and responded, "Well, I'm the broker and the president of the company, and I'm a she, and thanks because I do know my stuff about this real estate industry."

I picked up my glass of water, took a sip, and turned away. I knew right then, what would be my next steps. I was going to "pepper up" the real estate arena with women and people of color! Four months later, I started the Outreach School of Real Estate with its headquarters in the middle of the inner city of New Haven, CT. The School is licensed in Connecticut and eleven other reciprocal states across the country. As of 2019, the Outreach School of Real Estate has graduated hundreds of real estate professionals with a 99 percent minority enrollment. Most of the students enrolled in my school are from the Black and Latino ethnicities, with 80 percent of the students being women. However, my business creativity didn't stop there; it actually ignited.

I'll never forget the day I woke up to 112 messages and tags asking me questions about real estate investing. I had heard the fast-paced radio advertisement the day prior: Do you want to learn how to make a ton of money right here in the "Greater New Haven Area" flipping houses? We are looking for individuals to join our real estate investing team. We will show you how to flip properties with just two simple steps. Come to our free seminar tomorrow in downtown New Haven. This commercial upset me. I was angry that this group of real estate business owners would intentionally mislead people into thinking that flipping properties was a two-step process. I knew the only step that the attendees would learn at the free seminar was how to put more real estate deals in the pipeline of the investors. It was a clever marketing strategy, but it wasn't the most ethical strategy. This bothered me.

I logged on to my Facebook page to read question after question, but most of the questions started the same way. Some of the questions were: I went to a free real estate seminar last night and I...and I want to flip properties for an additional stream of income, but... I shook my head as I laid in bed because I felt the confusion of the people in my community that I love dearly. I knew they were being misled into thinking they could flip properties with only two steps. They may have had a suspicion that the concept was too good to be true, but I doubt they knew how much the seminar was designed to have them become real estate gophers for the company holding the seminar. It disgusted me. I spent the entire day answering every question to help correct the thinking of the way real estate investing is done.

That night, I couldn't sleep at all. I tossed and turned. God was speaking to me, and I had to listen. It was the same feeling I had when I started the Outreach School of Real Estate. It was a feeling that I just couldn't ignore. Two months later, I held my first Real Estate Investing Training in downtown New Haven. The room was filled above capacity. People were standing in the hallway listening to my training. I taught as if we were in school. I even had a question-and-answer segment during the training. This was definitely different from what people were accustomed to when they attended seminars. I discussed what broke poverty over my life. I taught how to flip properties, and it wasn't a two-step process. People left my training educated, not confused. The attendees were happy, and I was happy.

I don't know why I thought that the real estate investing training would be a onetime thing. I should have known better by now. At this point in my life, everything, I touched grew at a very rapid pace. I have been told that I have the "Midas Touch" and everything I touched had turned to gold. I understand the analogy, but I understand that what the world perceives as the "Midas Touch" is nothing more than "God's hands on my life" because I'm living "in my God-given purpose, and I'm doing it on purpose."

I pay close attention to my spirit, how it feels, and the timing of the things happening around me. When you understand the concept that whatever grieves you is an indicator of something you're designed to fix, then you will start being more productive. Apply this concept the next time you get emotional and don't understand why. Ask yourself, *"How can I create an equalizer to this negative emotion, instead of ignoring it?"*

Chapter Twenty-Eight

THE MILLIONAIRE NEXT DOOR

DEC. 23, 2014, I WAS featured on WFSB Channel 3 news in their "Rags to Riches" story. The story quickly went viral, from Connecticut to Hawaii, Canada, Bermuda, the UK, and beyond. I never thought WFSB Channel 3 would title the story, "New Haven Mother Uses Real Estate to Become a Millionaire." One thing the media is good at is quickly catching the attention of their audience. They certainly accomplished this, using this title and the content they shared.

I knew this article was divinely different. I couldn't explain the feeling that I had at the time. However, now, I understand it clearly. I know that a new level of accountability was placed on me the moment Channel 3 released the story. I had been told, since I was a little girl, more times than I can count that "Unto whom much is given, much is required." This Scripture, Luke 12:48, gained a new meaning and became the core of my being. I now know the feeling I felt was God's hand over my life. He was welcoming me to a new level, but not without new requirements.

God is very strategic about what He does and when He does it. Even though I was no longer on welfare, I left a six-figure job, I had a couple of successful businesses, and I no longer had a financial struggle; the thought that "I had made it," never entered my thought process. I never, ever thought, differently from the time when I started my business to the day of the news story.

I was in such a state of focus that I didn't realize when I had crossed over the line to prosperity and had left poverty behind me. I was never focused on prosperity, but instead, I was always focused on the "my purpose in life". So, when asked, "How did you do it?"; it puzzled me. Especially, after being asked the same question eight times within a two week time period. Even though I've been on television before, have had numerous articles written about me, and have won many awards, I didn't think I was doing anything different from anyone else. Until I was posed with the question "How did I do it?" over and over again.

My mother taught me to pay attention to the timing of things. So, I couldn't ignore the fact that this question was asked eight different times. At first, I gave a surface answer, and I told people what to do to invest in real estate. However, deep in my soul, I felt like I wasn't truly answering the question. I felt like I wasn't really helping them. This caused me to question myself.

I went into my prayer closet, in deep prayer and meditation. This prayer was an emotional one with tears streaming down my face at a rapid, uncontrollable pace. I was breathing heavy, almost to the point of hyperventilating. I prayed, *"Father, I feel like there is more to me. My heart aches, and cries for people I don't know. How can I help? What is this pull on my heart that I know not of? Why do I have this burden for people? Father, I know it is because of Your hand on my life, but there are countless worthy people in Your kingdom, and they are still fighting the battle that You delivered me from."* I paused. And then I asked God, "How did I do it? and Why me?"

How did I do it? The one question that was posed to me and that I had posed to God. Yes, I believe God is in the business of changing lives, but this was different. Why me? I thought about where many of my friends and family were in their lives. I thought of an old friend, and how she had been to my office looking for an apartment to rent and how it broke my heart that I was unable to help her due to the lack of money, numerous evictions, and her criminal record. The countless number of God-fearing people, including my mother, who were financially plagued. What made me different?

The easy way of thinking is to say, "God blessed me," which He did, but I'm no different from you, my family, my friends, or anyone who is reading this book. Yet, my life has drastically changed.

Why did financial freedom happen to me? I thought and here are the reasons I came up with:

1. Because everything belongs to God, my Father and I'm his child; the same is true for you. God is no more my Father than He is for anyone else. So, this answer didn't add up.

2. Because God gave me the desires of my heart; He will do that for everyone—not just me.

3. It was spoken into existence; but what about all of the worthy people who serve God that have been speaking financial blessings over their lives. Yet, their financial condition remains unchanged or only temporarily changed.

4. I was destined to be wealthy. I would agree to the point that God knew I would teach the world how to break poverty and write the book you're reading right now. However, it is God who gives the power to get wealth (Deuteronomy 8:18). The same power was given to us all—not just me.

5. I had Faith. Yes, this is true. Thoughts of not being successful never crossed my thought process even when it would be perceived that I had failed. However, if it was my faith, I personally know many people with much greater faith than I, including people of the Five-Fold ministries—Apostles, Pastors, Teachers, Evangelists, Prophets—but, they still battled with the poverty curse.

I was unable to pinpoint what had happened? Then, God spoke, "It was your mindset." *My mindset?* I thought.

Oh, God, never, did I think that it was my mindset. But, oh, it was the absolute truth.

Chapter Twenty-Nine

NOVEMBER 8TH—THE GOOD SAMARITAN

LITTLE DID I KNOW THAT Wednesday, November 8, 2017, was a day set *aside for God to change the course of my life totally, a gentleman by the name of Elmer Alvarez, and over fifty million people.*

It has been said that God works in mysterious ways and that He is in control over every detail in our lives—even when we are just carrying on with our normal day. It's important to know that God is definitely into the little details. When God has a message, He wants to communicate; He will do it in unconventional ways—in ways that you cannot deny the power of God.

This day forever changed the way I look at everyday encounters with everyday people and everyday situations. Make no mistake; God is orchestrating His perfect plan through imperfect people. The fact that you're even reading this book is part of His Plan. From this day forward, do not take things lightly because everything matters, and every "little" thing matters to God. God is in the details.

Beep, beep, beep, beep. With my eyes closed, I reached to grab my phone off the nightstand to silence my morning alarm. I opened my right eye to peak at the time; the clock read 6:00 a.m. "Fifteen more minutes, and then I'll get up," I muttered underneath my breath. I had to be in Naugatuck at 7:30 a.m. to pick up my commission check for the sale of my three-unit property located at 679 Winchester Avenue, New Haven. My partners and I were happy that we were finally closing since this property should have closed six months prior.

I had taken great pride in this property, and it was a gut rehab. When I first acquired the property, it looked as if it could barely stand. The front doors were nailed shut with plywood, dead mice laced the halls, the ugly brown paneling walls from the '70s were still erected, the popcorn ceilings had "popped," and were falling down, while large pieces of gray peeling paint were everywhere. It looked like a scene from a scary movie. I found it quite funny to see in the middle of this deplorable property that thirty-four empty bottles of Cîroc TM were neatly placed in the hutch as if they were being shown off as gold medals of achievement.

When walking into the first floor, we had to be very careful, since used drug needles, homemade crack pipes, and human feces covered the floor. The smell was unbearable, and it smelled as if a person's body had been decaying in the building for months. I had nearly vomited while gasping for air each time I had entered the building.

The bathrooms were filthy with a highly dysfunctional layout. The heating vent in the bathroom was in the middle of the shower wall that partly covered the bathroom window. The vanity was rotted, and someone's old tattered curly brown weave was still hanging out of the vanity drawer. I was able to see into the basement through the hole in the first-floor bathroom. The toilet was falling through the floor, and the subfloor was non-existent.

Many developers wouldn't have touched this project, but I was up for the challenge. When my team was finished, this long-time blighted house had turned into the best house on the street. It went from being a "hot mess" to being a "hot commodity" in the neighborhood. We had received multiple offers from people to acquire the property. We had offers from investors to purchase the house. However, I denied all of their offers. I was looking to give someone the opportunity that I had when I purchased my first home on 283

Norton Street, a four-family unit in New Haven. I wanted to pay it forward and create an opportunity for someone to get one step closer to financial freedom through the same steps of investing in an owner-occupied multi-family home, as I have done—but now I'm the one developing the houses.

I am not a morning person, so I wasn't happy about having an early appointment, but I didn't want the check to get lost in the mail due to my office recently moving to downtown New Haven. I turned over on my left side to hug my husband and attempted to go back to sleep. But… Beep, beep, beep, beep…it seemed like I had just hit the snooze button for that additional fifteen minutes and now, the phone was going off again. I took a big deep breath, hit the off button, and closed my eyes, once more.

During the three seconds of which my eyes were closed, I had a vision. I saw me holding my check and posting a picture of it on social media. I immediately jumped up and said out loud, "Now, that's stupid!" I stood up, took a nice long stretch, and proceeded to the bathroom to turn on the shower because it was time to start my day.

I dress the way I feel, and for some reason, I wanted to look pretty today. So, I took a little longer than normal to get ready for the day. I'm not a makeup girl, but I put on a little more than the usual amount of my MAC number 7.5 makeup this day. After an hour of preparation, I was in my car driving to Naugatuck. As I pulled up to my destination, I looked around, and everything looked as if it was trapped in the roaring '20s! Three and four-story brick and old stone buildings lined the street. The glass in the windows looked as though it had fifty years of layers of smog and smoke layered on them. It looked like the original windows were never upgraded, and these were the same windows from when the building was erected.

I struggled to open the heavy doors. The doors looked like they belonged on a castle, not on an attorney's office. They were metal and stood about ten feet tall, two feet thick, and extremely heavy to push open. I walked in the building to see a large thirty-five step, twenty feet wide stone staircase that led to the second floor. I felt like I was trespassing, and I was in the wrong building. So, I pulled out my phone to double check the address of my appointment. I was in the right place, and the attorney's office was on the third-floor. I climbed the stairs to the second-floor landing and looked at all of the pictures from the early '40s and '50s. At one time, this building was quite exquisitely built. It reminded me of the meticulously built municipal buildings that were built with great details, including gold trimmings and murals of the Greek god's painted on the ceilings.

I climbed the next set of stairs slowly, but surely. Trying hard to control my huffing and puffing from climbing the stairs, and to speak as normal as possible. I gathered my breath and said, "Hello. My name is Roberta Hoskie from Outreach Realty. I'm here to pick up a check." The thin woman with shoulder-length, straight, blonde hair smiled and grabbed the envelope from her "to be picked up" tray and said, "Yes, it's right here," and handed it to me. "Thank you," I said. I confirmed the amount of the check was for $10,800.00 and put it in my pocketbook. I proceeded back down the long flight of stairs, pushed the heavy door open, started my car, and headed to the office.

I drove in my car in circles for twenty-two minutes as there was what seemed to be utility construction going on, and the roads that Waze was directing me to take were closed. Therefore, I attempted to follow the bright burnt orange and black *detour* signs, which made me even more frustrated, as I drove in circles for several minutes. I felt my blood pressure rising, my tolerance level getting low, and the onset of road rage. Instead of acting out the thoughts in my head, which included constantly blowing the horn and screaming "Move" out the window like a maniac, I decided to stop at the Dunkin' Donuts ™ that I kept seeing in my peripheral vision on the right to reset my mindset.

I'm a firm believer that we have the ability to control the energy of our day. I knew that my energy was turning negative, and it was too early. I backed my car into the parking space, sat in the car in silence while watching the children in the neighborhood play at the bus stop, and walk with their book bags down the street. Then I started reminiscing how fast time flies by and remembered when my children were babies, bundled up, and going to the bus stop for school. I turned on my Pandora music to shift the atmosphere, and surely the song did it, as I sat alone in my car in the Dunkin' Donuts TM parking lot. I began to sing along with Bishop Paul Morton like I was singing to God, up close and personal!

In my best melody, I sang: "*How great is our God?* Sing with me. *How great is our God?* And all will see… How great… *How great is our God?* He is the name above all names, worthy of our praise, and my heart will sing *How great is our God!*"

Tears ran down my face as I got lost in praise with singing from my heart. The road rage and negative energy were surely gone, and just that fast, I was in a place of peace and happiness. "A medium, hot French vanilla cream, and three Splendas, please," I asked the cashier with a smile. The words from the song, *How Great is our God* continued to ring in the thoughts. "Sure, that will be $2.12," she replied. I handed her my phone with my Dunkin' Donuts TM app and paid for my order, then walked to the right and stood under the "pick up" sign patiently awaiting my morning coffee. "Here's your French vanilla cream with two Splendas," she said as she handed me the coffee. "Do you mean three Splendas?" I replied. "Oh, you said two Splendas," she insisted.

Now, the devil knows how to test me. One of my biggest pet peeves is when someone tries to tell me what I said. So, I saw this for what it was, and I was determined to stay in a *happy place* today. "I said three, but it's okay. May I have a couple of extras?" I said. She handed me three little, yellow packets of Splenda. I went to the table to taste the coffee, and it tasted like there wasn't any sweetener in it at all, so I put all three Splendas in my coffee. I went back to my car, took a deep breath, began to sing, started my car, and focused on not driving into circles and getting back to my office.

Pulling up to my office wasn't the same as it was when my office was on Whalley Avenue. I had my own parking space, and I didn't have to battle for a parking space. Having my office located downtown had its pro's, but it definitely had its challenges, and parking was one of the main challenges. After circling the office four times and listening to drivers beep their car horns and holler like maniacs, I finally saw a person leaving from their parking spot. I put on my left signal and waited for the space, forcing myself to look at the positive. I was happy to have found a space on this side of the office building. I chose to ignore the road rage, negative people, the conflicts I just saw in my schedule, and that it was my mother's birthday and I hadn't gotten her a gift, yet. I grabbed my initialed computer bag, my pocketbook, a stack of files that I was returning, took a picture of the meter code, and headed to the office.

"Tenth floor, please," I asked the gentleman in the elevator with me. "Tenth floor, it is," he said in an upbeat, happy tone. I smiled as I got off the elevator and walked into my office. "Hello, Sarah." "Good morning, Roberta." "Hello, Ms. Jonnell." "Hello, Boss Lady." I sat down at the desk facing the window and pulled out my laptop to start my day.

"Did you make it to Naugatuck this morning?" Sarah jokingly asked. Sarah knows that I'm not a morning person. She knows me well since she has been the office manager for over five years. "Yes, I rolled on out of bed, and I was there on time. I wasn't going to be late with picking up money," I said in a jokingly fashion. We both laughed.

I dug in my bag looking for the envelope with the check. When I didn't see it in my bag, I checked my pocketbook, but it wasn't there, either. *I must have left it in the car,* I thought to myself. So, I grabbed my pocketbook, put my coat on, and proceeded to go to my car to retrieve it. As soon as I went out of the office, I was startled as Sarah urgently banged on the window to get my attention. Sarah had the office phone to her ear and motioned for me to come back. I turned around and opened the office door.

"There's a guy on the phone, saying that he has your check," Sarah said in an urgent and serious tone. "My check? Where is he?" I quickly responded. "He said that he is downstairs in front of the coffee shop." "Okay, come on, Jonnell," I said. Jonnell grabbed her coat, and we rushed out of the office to meet the gentleman who was kind enough to call the office to return my check.

As we walked off from the elevator and outside to downtown New Haven, I took out my phone and went to Facebook live and typed, "This guy found my check for over 10k." I wanted to showcase the good Samaritan, and I wanted to show that there are still very good people in this world.

The numbers on my Facebook live viewers were extremely high. I continued going through downtown with Jonnell while Facebook live was recording. I had no idea what the good Samaritan looked like. I assumed he would be a clean-cut, financially well-off businessman working in the downtown area. Then I thought, he may have been an attorney because attorneys normally hold a high value on being ethical. I expected to see a man in a wool coat, custom suit, white shirt with a tie and shiny brown shoes. But instead, the man I saw didn't have a wool coat, but a red and once was a white coat that was three sizes too big. No, he didn't have a custom suit, he had jeans too big with holes at the bottom from walking on them. No, he didn't have shiny brown shoes; he had worn sneakers that were two sizes too big. Never did I think that the gentleman who was returning my check for over $10,000 was a man who was homeless!

When he shared with me that he was homeless, I was immediately overwhelmed with so many mixed emotions—I was confused, happy, and sad—all at the same time and the confusion showed all over my face. "You're homeless?" I asked. "Yes," Elmer's friend answered for him. "He doesn't speak much English. He asked me to help him find you because he had to return the check to you," he continued. "Wow," I said, as I shook my head in amazement. "Do you think you can help him out?" he asked. I shook my head up and down and said, "Sure. Absolutely. I was planning on writing him a check before you asked. I just have to go up to my office and get a check." "Thank you. Thank you," Elmer said. "Do you have ID so that you can cash the check?" I asked.

Elmer dug in his pocket and pulled out his wallet to show me a copy of his driver's license. The picture on the license looked totally different from the man I was looking at. I looked twice to confirm it was him, and it was. Based on the picture of him on his license, it was clear that he was newly homeless and that he was now accustomed to this lifestyle. He looked happy, shaved, well-dressed, and clean-cut on the photo. "Okay, stay right here, and I'll be right back," I said. I began to walk away, but then I turned around and asked, "What made you decide to return my check?" He pointed to his heart and then to the sky and responded, "Porque si haces lo correcto por Dios, él hará lo correcto por ti." His friend translated what Elmer had said, "He said because if you do the right thing for God, he will do the right thing for you." His friend further explained, "And he believes in God." When these words came from his mouth, my spirit leaped, and I knew that this was all God!

"Yes, God," I said. "I feel you," I said underneath my breath and began to walk back to the office. "Can you believe that, Jonnell?" "Was the office number on the check?" "No, they had to Google the office." "So, they had to put in some work," Jonnell said. "Can you believe this? Of all people to find the check, it ends up being a homeless person! I have to figure out how to bless him." "Jonnell, can you go upstairs and get me a blank check? I'm going to stay in the lobby because I don't want to lose the people on my live feed in the elevator." "Okay," she said.

Still overwhelmed with emotion, I paced back and forth in the main lobby, trying to figure out how to help Mr. Alvarez. There was such a sense of urgency that I began to ask the people who were on the live feed to strategize with me on how to help him. As I waited for Jonnell to come back with the check, I interacted with the people of Facebook live and began reading their suggestions. Someone suggested, "Give him an apartment." I responded with, "If we find him an apartment, at some point, he will need to sustain it." Another suggested, "Give him money." Another suggestion read, "Teach him to fish." My eyes got big, "Yes, Real Estate School. I'm going to teach him to fish!" Not only did this suggestion make sense to create sustainability, but it was an ancient proverb that also reflects biblical principles.

"Give a man a fish, and he will eat for the day, but teach a man to fish, and he will eat all his days" (Wiktionary contributors 2019).

I was excited. I couldn't wait to tell him the good news that I was going to show and train him how to "fish." Jonnell returned to the lobby with two blank checks. I quickly wrote Elmer Alvarez a check and then I wrote the gentleman that helped him a check for his role in the return of my check. Rushing, Jonnell and I go back outside near the coffee shop to see the two men waiting for my return. As I was walking towards him, I felt God's presence overtake me. He began to cry, and I began to testify of how God had brought me from "poverty to prosperity" and how God had broken the "poverty curse" over my life.

I put my arm around him and began to speak from my heart. I said, "It pays to do the right thing. I don't even know who you are, but I thank God for you. I don't care what your situation is, but God has His hand all over your life. Whatever, you're going through, it's temporary. You continue to do the right thing, and I am going to help you. I have a real estate school. My company teaches people how to sell real estate and make the big commission checks like the one you found. I am willing to let you come to my school for free, as someone on my Facebook live feed said for me to teach you how to fish. This is what I'm going to do. I'm going to teach you how to fish. But, what you do not know is that I was once homeless. So, God knows what to do and when to do it. So, when I tell you that your situation is temporary, I'm not just talking to be talking."

Emotionally charged, for a moment, I forgot I was on Facebook Live when I began to what some people would call ministering to Mr. Alvarez. I saw a person with a good heart, a person who chose to do the right thing. I saw a child of God. I didn't see a homeless man. I didn't see a hopeless man. I saw a child of God. There is an old saying that "actions speak louder than words" held true in my encounter with Mr. Alvarez. There are so many people in this world, who profess to live according to the Bible and other religious books, who do not show forth compassion or honesty the way that Mr. Alvarez did. His actions spoke volumes, and it spoke to my heart.

Elmer was a reminder to me of a prayer and promise I gave to God when I was a little girl. I prayed, "Father, bless me so that I can be a blessing to others." God truly held up His promise to me as I was in a position to "lose" a check for $10,000 check and not even know it! Now, it was time to be a blessing to Mr. Alvarez. I had already blessed Mr. Alvarez and his friend with a nice check. However, I couldn't rest until I gave him all of the tools that he needed to break the poverty over his life. I had been tossing and turning for nights, asking God what I should do? God finally answered and said, "bless him".

Two weeks later, on the Wednesday before Thanksgiving, I held a press conference and invited local and national media that I had previously interviewed to participate in the surprise I had planned for Elmer. I made a Facebook posting alerting all of my following to tune in as I would show, "How Thanksgiving should be done!"

Lisha in my office, coordinated with Elmer to arrive at my office at 9:30 a.m. The media arrived an hour and a half before Elmer arrived to set up their cameras and lighting. I felt calm and at peace that what I was about to do was God's Work.

I met with Elmer a week prior to do some fact-finding. I wanted to know what caused him to be in his homeless state, and how could I help him. Many people told me to give him money, but I knew that money was a temporary solution for him and a "band-aid" to his problem. I didn't want a "band-aid," I wanted a solution. After doing my fact-finding, I worked hard to put a package of solutions together for him, and since the media was in need of some good news, I was going to give it to them.

After the media was ready, Elmer arrived to be surprised by cameras and people clapping and giving him a standing ovation. Elmer was startled since he thought he was going to be meeting with just me and not walking into a room with cameras pointing at him. I reached out and hugged him.

I began by saying, "Two weeks ago, you found my check for over $10,000, and you did the right thing and returned it. Many people would not have made that decision, but you did. So, because of this, I told you that I was going to help you, and today, I am a woman of my word." Lisha handed me the folder with the items I was going to bless him with. I opened the folder and read each item to Elmer, one-by-one while the media recorded the event.

"When we met last week, you shared your desire to have stronger communication skills when speaking English. So, in this folder, you will find the name of a person whom we have spoken to and is waiting on your call. She teaches English as a Second Language. You also stated that you were in the middle of a legal battle that has contributed to your homeless status. So, in this folder, you will find the name and contact number of an attorney who is waiting for your call. She is ready, willing, and able to help you as needed, free of charge.

Also, you will find in this folder, a full scholarship to the Outreach School of Real Estate, and we will train you to start a new career as a real estate salesperson. We want you to start generating the checks like the one you found. You explained that you previously worked as a carpenter. So, I have a phone number of one of my colleagues who owns a construction company, and he is ready to put your hands to work, whenever you are ready. And Last, but certainly not least, you don't have to worry about being in the cold this winter, we have housing for you." Elmer erupted in tears of gratitude to God and to me. His prayers were answered—all because he did the right thing.

I believe that God is constantly testing us on a daily basis. I remembered my promise to God that if He would bless me, then I would be a blessing to others. My life has gone full circle—from being a single teenage mother on welfare, receiving $417 per month, and homeless to losing a $10,000 plus check and not even noticing! The poverty curse was broken over my life, and now, I was able to pay it forward and to give someone else the opportunity to break poverty over their life.

Over the next few weeks, our story of love and compassion went worldwide.

Chapter Thirty

Antigua, Country of Cyprus, Telemundo Worldwide, China, and Russia—the prophecy was fulfilled all on the same day within a three-hour time frame.

"Roberta, wait one minute," the receptionist said as she covered the phone. I had a late start to my day. Therefore, I was walking briskly past her desk to get my afternoon cup of coffee. "I saw you on television in Antigua last night. When I saw you come across the screen, I started screaming, I know her!" I must have had a strange look on my face. I was trying to figure out how I'm talking to her in New Haven, and she saw me in Antigua last night. "I'm from Antigua, so I still watch their television stations," she said. "Wow, to God be the Glory," I said as I took my right hand, tapped my heart two times, and pointed to the heavens. "To God be the Glory," she smiled and further said, "God is up to something." "Yes, He is," I responded. I put both of my hands in the air, praising God as I continued my walk to the office kitchen to prepare my coffee.

Wow, God. You're just amazing, I thought to myself. I quietly praised God back to my office. I was in an unusually good mood today after having an unusual morning prayer. My Millionaire Mindset Sister, Kay, had lost her dad two days before, and this morning, I was overwhelmed with discerning my sister's grief. So, I did what I knew best, and that was to pray. That prayer started with Kay and ended with prayers for my friend, family, and the people of the entire world. I knew this was a special day, so I expected God to move.

Many times, when we are going through issues in life, we need to start expecting God to move in our life. "Lisha, are my appointments for today confirmed?" I asked as I entered the office. "Yes, Dr. Hoskie all confirmed," Lisha, my new assistant, said. We were in a temporary office space waiting for my office to be ready to move into by the end of that week. We were sharing a large conference room overlooking the New Haven Green. We may have been a bit uncomfortable sharing space, but we had the best view in the building from the tenth floor. I pulled out my laptop and logged in.

The internet was so slow, it was driving me insane, and to control my dissatisfaction, I shifted my focus; I picked up my phone and logged on to Facebook. Since the story of Elmer and I had hit, my message box was inundated with messages. So much so that Facebook started filtering the messages. The messages were from people near and far—men, women, boys, and girls—some I knew and some I will never know.

A message from a man named Mehmet Akkent stood out to me among all of the other messages. Maybe, it was his profile picture that drew my curiosity—a black background with a bright yellow shape that looked like a shield, which was outlined in hunter green with the initials MTG in the shield. On top of the yellow and green symbol were two yellow stars. I didn't know the meaning of this symbol, but it caught my attention. I clicked on the filtered message, and it had two words and a link to a picture. The two words were "bravo layd." I had no idea what this meant. With my curiosity rising, I clicked on the link. *Maybe the pictures will have more of an explanation of why I am receiving this message, I thought.*

The internet was still working slow, so I looked at a circle as I waited for it to download. Finally! It was on the cover of a local Newspaper. It read, "10 bin *dolarlik, ceki sahibine verdi, evle odullendirildi.*" "Huh? What the heck is this?" I couldn't understand it. The newspaper was from a different country. Why would someone send me a copy of a foreign newspaper that I can't even read? But before I clicked the link to exit out of my messenger, I saw bright green in a picture on the cover bottom right. It was a familiar picture. It was a picture of Elmer and I at the press conference I held for him the week before!

In a somewhat frantic way, I immediately started investigating who Mehmet Akkent was and what part of the world he was from. I looked closely at his Facebook profile to find out he was the CEO of Aspava Restaurants located in Magusa, Famagusta, in the Country of Cyprus! "Lisha, Sarah, look at this," I turned my phone around to show them the article. "Cyprus, where in the world is Cyprus?" I said.

Sarah turned to her desktop and typed it in Google, "Where is the country of Cyprus?" Then she turned in her chair with an expression of amazement, "Look," she said as she pointed at the screen and continued, "It's a little island off the coast of Turkey!" My mouth dropped with surprise. Lisha and I locked eyes and her expression mirrored mine. "God is up to something," Lisha said. "He sure is," I responded. "This is weird," Sarah said.

I knew right then and there that God was setting me up. For what, I didn't know, but He has my face and story on the cover of the newspapers on the other side of the world. I kept staring at the article as if I was decoding a mystery. After all, the Bible says that God works in mysterious ways! I took a screenshot photo and posted it on my personal Facebook page with the following comment: *"Look at what someone messaged me. I'm on the cover of the newspaper in Magusa, Famagusta, in the country of Cyprus! Look at God Move!"*

Immediately, Facebook friends and followers began to respond. *Lord, I don't know what You're doing, show me why You are allowing this simple story to go viral,* I thought. I stirred my coffee, and it was awful. I went scrambling through my desk looking for my stash of little yellow packets of Splenda. I had started collecting Splenda packets ever since my husband was diagnosed with Type II Diabetes. I had changed my eating habits to help him, so I no longer ate sugar. After digging in my black pocketbook with the three-inch big tassel, I found my little yellow packet. I poured it in, stirred my coffee again, and now it was perfect. "Let me get to work," I said out loud. Talking to myself had become far too common lately, but for some reason, it was helpful to me to maintain my focus. I rolled my neck around and moved my shoulders in a circle rotation, in an attempt to relax and shift my mindset from what had just happened. I took a deep breath and proceeded to open my email, and I began to scan the subject lines. I scanned because of the high volume of marketing emails so close to the holiday. I saw a headline that read, *"Telemundo Network: Don Francisco* Show." I clicked on the email subject at once. My eyes opened wide, and I put my hand over my mouth as I read the email.

Good Afternoon Roberta,

My name is Massiel Ojito Producer for the show, "Don Francisco te Invita." I'm reaching out to you because of the homeless story, I saw on the news. It is a beautiful gesture what he did and also what you did for him. I would love to connect with you and with Elmer and then propose the story to the general producer for the show to invite you both to our program.

"Don Francisco te Invita show" airs every Sunday on Telemundo at 10:00 a.m. Eastern Time. It is hosted by Mario Kreutzberger, better known as Don Francisco, who is very well known among the Hispanic community due to his iconic show, Sabado Gigante, running for almost 54 years on TV.

Here is a link to our show http://www.telemundo.com/shows/don-francisco-te-invita

Looking forward to hearing from you.

Kindly Regards
Massiel Ojito
Senior Producer Don Francisco Te Invita

My God, My God, what are you doing? I said out loud. I immediately responded to the email. Hello, thank you for reaching out to me. My assistant Lisha will be in contact with you. Then, I spun around in my chair and said, "Lisha, I just forwarded you a request from Telemundo, call them right now." Before I finished speaking,

Lisha picked up the phone, and began dialing the phone number in the email from Massiel.

"Hello, my name is Lisha, and I am the Assistant to Dr. Roberta Hoskie. I'm responding to the email that was sent regarding the Don Francisco Te Invita Show." "Thank you for responding so quickly. I read the story about the homeless guy who returned her $10,000 check. We would like to have Roberta and Elmer on the show in December. I would like to do a phone interview with Roberta so that I can pitch the show to the producers," she said.

Lisha put her hand over the telephone receiver and signaled to me by pointing to the phone and having me read her lips. "She wants to talk to you now," she mouthed. I vigorously shook my head, indicating "yes." "Okay, Massiel, let me see if Dr. Hoskie is available to speak with you now," Lisha said.

She then transferred the call to me as I sat right across the room. "Hello, this is Roberta speaking," I said. In a heavy Spanish accent, the woman responded, "Hello, Roberta. What a wonderful thing you did for that guy. It's such a lovely story, and you don't hear these types of nice things anymore. I saw your Facebook live video, and I shared it on my page. God bless you." "Thank you. Thank you," I said. "So, you didn't know you lost the check?" she questioned in amazement.

"No, I didn't. I thought it was in my car."

"When did you find out the check was missing?"

"I knew I had the check, and I was on my way out of the door to go when my assistant, Sarah, banged on the window to get my attention." She said, "There's a guy on the phone who says he has your check." "Wow," she continued, "My understanding is that you helped him get English classes and gave him a full scholarship to your real estate school." "Yes, we also gave him a check, a job interview and made sure he's not out in the cold this winter," I responded.

"This is such an awesome story. We want you and Elmer to be guests on our show. I would like to speak with Elmer, first, and then I will confirm and provide you with the date and time of the show. Of course, we will pay for your travel and hotel accommodations. We are thinking that we would like to have you both come on in a couple of weeks, possibly in mid-December," she explained. "Okay, great. I will get in touch with Elmer, now, and have him reach out to you," I said. "Great, I look forward to the call," she said.

I hung up the phone. I stared out of the window in amazement of what had just happened. Then, I said in a calm, controlled voice, "Lisha, please get Elmer on the phone and ask him to call Massiel at Telemundo." I lifted my head toward the heavens and said, "Father, I thank you for what you are doing. I thank you, Lord, for opening this door," with my hands lifted up as Lisha dialed Elmer's phone number.

After two attempts, she looked at me with a sad expression on her face, she said no words, but I heard the words, "The phone is disconnected." So, I said, "The phone is disconnected," as if she had just uttered those tragic words out of her mouth. "Yes," she said as she hung her head, and then added, "But wait, he called from a different number two days ago, and something told me to write it down."

Lisha dialed the number from a few days ago. "Whose number is it?" I asked. "I think it's his girlfriend's number." A woman answered the call. "Hello, this is Lisha from Outreach Realty. We are looking for Elmer." "Hold on," the woman said as she put Elmer on the phone. "Hello." "Hello, Elmer. This is Lisha, and Dr. Roberta would like to speak with you briefly." "Okay." "Hi, Elmer. How have you been doing?" I said. "Good," he said.

"Have you given your caseworker the approval to talk to me, yet?"

"Yes, I was there yesterday, and she has all that she needs."

"Did you decide if you want to contact the person for employment, or did you want to fight for your disability?" I asked.

"Ms. Roberta, I want to work," he responded.

"Good, well, contact the contractor. He is waiting for your call," I said.

"Thank you so much, Ms. Roberta. You're such a Blessing."

"Awww... To God be the Glory," I said, and added, "I have some good news for you," I said. "Telemundo wants us to be guests on the Don Francisco Show!" Immediately, I heard screaming and praising to God from Elmer and his girlfriend. It was so loud that I could hear it through the phone. Lisha stopped what she was doing and remained in dead silence as she was moved by compassion. I put the phone on speaker so that she could clearly hear their responses. "Thaaaaaaank yooooooou, Jeeeeeeeeesus. Thaaaaaaaaank yooooooou Jeeeeeeeeesus," they repeatedly said in between their weeping.

Finally, Elmer said, "Thank you, Roberta, you're an angel, you're an angel from the heavens. Thank you, Roberta, you're a good woman." I could tell that he was crying and could only imagine the tears that flowed down his face as he looked up to the heavens. I knew that he was humbled as he felt God's presence in his life.

"Thank God, Elmer, not me. I'm just the pawn for Him," I said. "But, Roberta, many people wouldn't do what you did for me. You have a good heart," Elmer replied in his strong Spanish accent. I smiled, tapped my heart three times, and pointed to the heavens. "To God be the Glory," I said. "Lisha is about to text Massiel's contact information. Call her, now, and then call me back," I said. "Okay, okay, I'm calling, now," Elmer said.

We hung up the phone. I looked at Lisha, and tears were filling up in her eyes.

"Thank you, Lord," I said as I shook my head. "Telemundo. This is a Worldwide Network. God, what are you doing?" I said out loud.

I left the office, walked to the bathroom that was shared by the other tenants in the building. I hoped no one was in the bathroom since I wanted to be alone. At the moment, I was overwhelmed by God's spirit, and anyone who may have entered that bathroom may not have understood what was happening.

I stood in front of the newly cleaned mirrors, leaned on the sink, looked at myself eye-to-eye in the mirror and said, "Father, I don't know what You're doing, but it's big, and I am ready," as tears rolled uncontrollably down my face. With my head hung, tears still flowing, and both of my hands raised in surrender, I said,

"Lord, here I am, here I am. I will go where You send me, and I will say what You tell me to say. Father, here I am."

After five minutes, I carefully wiped my face. I needed to use wisdom—everyone in the building didn't need to know that I was crying. Everyone doesn't understand the movement of God, especially in the workplace—so, I used wisdom. I walked out of the bathroom, back to my office with my head up, a pep in my step, and a smile on my face, like God just didn't break me down to pieces in the bathroom (I'm sure some of you may have had this type of experience, as well.).

I calmly sat down at the desk to finish reading my emails.

Chapter Thirty-One

MORE TO COME

"DING," IN MY PERIPHERAL VISION, I saw a Facebook message alert on my cell phone, which was located face up on the desk next to the computer keyboard. I had been receiving messages all week from people from all over the world, who had read the story in the paper or saw it on the news. Therefore, I knew this message was from another kind-hearted person from across the world and that I would get back to them after I had finished going through my emails. Trying to ignore this message was an internal fight that I lost!

So, I grabbed the phone and read the message. The message read: *Hello, Roberta. I saw your story on the local news. I have a radio show that I would love to have you on as a guest. Please, contact me to discuss it.* I copied the message and pasted it into a text message to Lisha, and I asked her to call the contact because I wanted to do the show. I continued to read and respond to my emails.

"Dr. Hoskie, I spoke to the woman that wants you to be a guest on her radio show. We are all set for the pre-interview next week, and here is the call-in information," Lisha said as she handed me the link with what I perceived as a non-US phone number. "Where does this show air?" I asked. "Russia," she responded. Stunned, I repeated, "Russia?" "Yes, Russia, and they will provide an interpreter," Felicia said.

I sat at my desk and just shook my head and stared out of the window, knowing that God is moving in a mighty way. I took a deep breath and went back to answering emails. "Ding," Facebook Messenger alerted me that I had another message. At this point, I was barely able to concentrate, so I just grabbed the phone and read the message.

The message read: *I was moved by your story of the homeless man finding your check. I understand that you too, were homeless. This is a powerful story. Please contact me. I would like to have you as a guest on my radio show.*

"Lisha, another radio show just reached out. Here's the information. Please, schedule them." "Okay, I'll contact them now." "Hello, I'm calling on behalf of Dr. Roberta Hoskie." I heard Lisha say in the background. I definitely wasn't used to sharing an office, but I only had one more week to go until my private office was ready. I'm sure Lisha and Sarah were counting the days as well.

I heard the phone hang up. Lisha turned in her seat and looked at me with a look of astonishment. "What?" I asked. Lisha began to speak as she walked toward me with a piece of paper in her hand. "Well, you are all set with your radio interview, here is the call-in information," she said as she handed me a piece of paper again with unfamiliar numbers. "Where is this show aired?" I asked. "China and they will have an interpreter," Lisha responded. "China?" I grabbed my head, shook it, closed my eyes, and took in three deep breaths. I grabbed my pocketbook off the window seal, my coat from around the back of my seat, and without a word, I silently walked to my car.

My staff knew not to ask any questions as they were also seeing first-hand the mysterious work of God. While waiting for the elevator, silent tears began to roll down my face, but my mouth couldn't utter a word—not even a hello to the people in the elevator when it arrived or the people I passed on the way to my car. Even the drive home on the highway was silent—no Music, no talking—complete silence.

I got off at exit sixty-five—this is the exit I always take to come home. I don't remember all of the turns it took to bring me home. It was as if I was in a light daze. I pulled into my driveway and pushed my garage door opener. My garage door, the third one to the right opened, and I drove in. I grabbed my pocketbook, my laptop bag, went into my home, and walked straight to my bedroom. I dropped my items on the ottoman. I walked straight to my office, grabbed an index card with the Millionaire Mindset logo on it, and then proceeded to walk to the back of my twenty-foot closet. I pulled out my gray velvet pillow with the cream color cross from the shelf, put it on the floor, and sat on it Indian style with my palms raised up toward the heavens. I took three deep breaths and closed my eyes. I said, *"Lord, here am I."*

I didn't bombard heaven with a lot of words as I knew God knew exactly what I was looking for. He was up to something, and I wanted to know, so I would be sure I was ready for whatever he would bestow upon me.

After about fifteen minutes of prayer, I was overtaken by God's Spirit. I felt strong tingles throughout my entire body, from the top of my head to the soles of my feet. I was rocking back and forth in my closet, meditating in God's Blessings.

Then I began to write: *Remind them that God is real.* Many people give God lip service, and it is time to be real. He is looking for vessels ready and willing that will serve Him not for what He can do, but for who He is. So, He had sent a clear reminder that this world is His playground.

In one day, He had the administrative person from Antigua contact me, a Person from the Country of Cyprus, a worldwide television network, a radio station that airs in China, and one that airs in Russia. The message from God was very clear: *Let everyone know it's time to love one another and to put aside every weight. The time is winding near—Jesus is Coming!*

I dropped my pen, put my face in my hands, rocked back and forth, and said, once again with tears streaming down my face, "Lord, here I am." I stood up, stretched my arms toward heaven, grabbed my phone out of my pocketbook. I went to the Facebook app with my hands shaking, and I made a posting at 7:14 p.m.: *OMG! I'll be live at 7:30 p.m... Tune in, and please share... God is Moving* ♡*!*

I gave myself fifteen minutes to praise and worship God before delivering the message He had given me.

I prayed, "Lord, I thank You for Your word. Lord, when my mouth opens to talk on Facebook live, don't let it be me. Oh, Lord, let it be You—None of me, All of You."

I went into my bathroom, looked in the mirror, grabbed the white washcloth that was hanging on the side of the linen closet. I put some warm water on it, washed my face, combed my hair, and put some lip gloss on. I picked up the phone, logged onto Facebook, and in the status bar, I typed: *God is speaking, and I can't ignore it!*

I was pacing back and forth in my bedroom—from right to left, and from left to right. I nervously said, "Okay, God, let's do it! Here I am." I knew what God wanted me to deliver on the live feed. I was overflowing with emotion and enthusiasm. I looked at my phone, clicked the start live video. It was time to deliver, I thought, as I watched the timer countdown from five to one before my video would be aired live on Facebook.

> *Hey, hey, hey everyone. Woooo, Wwwwee. I got something to say, TODAY! Come on and jump on the live feed and please share it. Everybody that gets on this live feed, I want you to share it. I'm going to give you a few minutes to jump on and share it. Share it, share it, share it. I really need you to share it.*

I proceeded to call out the names of the people whom I saw getting on the live feed, and I began asking them to share the video. I had asked people to share my videos before but not this intentional. For the first four minutes, I was asking, requesting, and telling the viewers to share the video.

> *God wants to remind people that He is so real. Many people have been giving God a lot of lip service— just talking. As I picked up my notes, I said, I'm reading this because I have to get this straight. I continued, many people are giving God lip service,*

but He's looking for people who are real. He is looking for those who are ready, willing, and able. He is looking for people who will serve Him, not for what He can do for them, but just for who He is. Yes, God is looking for people, the real people of God to stand up. Stop having lip service, and be in position, not for what He can do for you, but because of who He is! God made it very clear to me today…very, very clear, in fact, crystal clear. I took a deep breath and said, *Let me tell you my testimony.*

My day started with unusual praise and prayer. I began to pray for people all across the world, including people that I know and people that I do not know. I even prayed for my enemies, my haters, and all of those people.

When I got to work today, in my new office, one of the administrative assistants stopped me and said, Roberta, I saw you on the news in Antigua, I'm from Antigua, and I still watch their news, so I was excited to see you. Then, shortly thereafter, I went to my computer, and I posted a picture from a guy that had a picture of me on the cover of a newspaper with a circle that said, 'Only God' from the Country of Cyprus! I didn't even know where Cyprus was until today. It's a little island, next to Turkey. So, this brown girl's picture is on the cover of a newspaper in a different country in a different language.

Next, I got an email from the Telemundo, the Worldwide Television Network, wanting me to do a talk show! It does not stop there, a few minutes later, I get another request, to do a radio show in China, and shortly thereafter, another request came in for me to do another radio show, but this time in Russia! This is ALL Today! My God, My God!

From Antigua to the Country of Cyprus to Telemundo's Worldwide Network to China to Russia, and ALL in one day!

Now, I'm going to tell you what God's doing, and I'm sorry, but I have to be obedient. If you didn't share this video, you need to share it. In a snap, God has elevated—not just national, not international, but Worldwide! The reason is that He has a message that I am carrying; a message that I am carrying in my bosom (a message that He wants to let the entire world know), and I'm going to deliver that message. I'm going to deliver it the way that I have received it, and it's a simple message. God is saying to let everyone know that it is time to love one another, it is time to put aside every weight, and it is time to worship Him because 'time is winding up! The only reason why my story went all over the world is that God has set it up to be so. There is nobody that can tell me any different! There is nobody that can deny the Power of God coming through this video, right now! We have to love one another; we have to have a deeper level of compassion! The reason why my story went viral is that I showed what Jesus Christ showed—I showed what true Christianity is. It's about love, it's about compassion, and it's about helping thy neighbor. We have too much hate and too many haters around here! We need to get our stuff together. I have never been the person to say, 'Jesus is coming back'. I have never been that person!

The reason why He put me in all of those places is that I have a big ole mouth and I'm going to tell it! I'm going to tell it! For God, I live. For God, I Will Die! Share this video.

Then, I hit the finish live video button. I sat on the edge of my bed and rocked back and forth.

Chapter Thirty-Two

FULL CIRCLE

MY QUEST TO BREAK THE "poverty curse" over my life began when I realized that my son's life was directly depended on mine. The day I realized I had nothing to offer him, except poverty and what goes along with it. This was the sole reason that I pushed so hard to better myself, and to become a better mother and person.

I've learned countless lessons about life along this journey. I learned that "fear" can be transformed into "faith". Faith is invisible, but it can create the visible. I had enough faith that if I worked hard on me, then my son would directly benefit. Today, my son that I gave birth to in poverty is the youngest faculty member at a prominent private school in Connecticut, where he teaches English. He is also, one of the few African American Faculty members on staff and he coaches varsity football. Dante never rented an apartment; he left his mother's home and became a homeowner with substantial equity at age twenty-five. He mentors countless boys, young and old, some of whom come from challenged family backgrounds, and are plagued with what he was made free of—the poverty curse. Oliver and Allia are both in College, in preparation to step into their inheritance as heirs of the Family Real Estate Empire.

When reading my story, you may have seen parts of your story. Know that everything is for a reason and that it is in your *struggle* and your *pain* that you will identify your *power* and *purpose* that God has for you to fulfill. When you understand this concept, you will no longer feel like life is "happening" to you, but you will make *life happen* for you.

Along with my journey, I found out that God has placed in each and every one of us a *power* that is more powerful than we can imagine. And that is the *power* of the *ability* to think things into existence. Everything that was ever created was created to solve a problem. Airplanes, cars, and trucks were created to solve transportation problems. School, universities, and colleges were created to solve educational problems. The telephone was created to solve communication problems, and the list goes on. Understand that everything that was ever created was created twice, first in our mindset then secondly in the world.

What is it that you are designed to do? What problems did or do you have to overcome in life? What are you hiding from? The thing that you are hiding from may be the thing that will set your free.

As I continue to speak and share my testimony all over the world, I will always encourage people to look at the problems and find the strength in it. Don't be ashamed of your life and what happened to you. Use it to ignite your power and the ability to set others free. In the end, it's not about you, but it's about the God in you. If God allowed it to happen to you, understand it was for a reason and such a time as this.

BE FREE,
BE REAL,
BE POWER,
BE THE CHANGE,
BE THE TRENDSETTER,

and most of all, BE ALL that God Designed you to be. Today, declare that "The Poverty Curse is Broken".

Ms. Millionaire Mindset
Sisterhood

When you know why God allows you to breathe, things become quite different for you. You become laser focused, intentional, and fearless. When you know that God has ordained you for a purpose, a boldness will reveal itself, and you will understand. What God has ordained, no one, nowhere can contain. This is my mindset.

I will live every breathing moment of my life devoted to raising the Greatness Sisterhood this world has ever seen! An International Faith Based Sisterhood of Women from all walks of life, in seven continents, devoted to breaking the poverty curse. A Sisterhood that thinks and plans for generational wealth. A Sisterhood that exemplifies the power of unity, loyalty, and group economics. A Sisterhood that will outlive all its Founders and me. When I sat at the Conference room table, for my first planning meeting, I said, "Now, let's plan for 100 years out."

The Sisterhood that I speak about is the Millionaire Mindset Sisterhood. It arose on April 15, 2017, and will continue to rise until God has the earth no more.

When you know why you breathe; things become different, and so do you. "It's time to *Break the Poverty Curse*!"

With Love, Hope and Vision,
Dr. Roberta A Hoskie
Founder and Chieftain of the Global
Millionaire Mindset Sisterhood.

References

The Holy Bible: New International Version [NIV]. 1984. Grand Rapids: Zondervan Publishing House.

Wiktionary contributors, "give a man a fish and you feed him for a day; teach a man to fish, and you feed him for a lifetime," *Wiktionary, The Free Dictionary,* https://en.wiktionary.org/w/index.php?title=give_a_man_a_fish_and_you_feed_him_for_a_day;_teach_a_man_to_fish_and_you_feed_him_for_a_lifetime&oldid=52542232

About the Author

ROBERTA A. HOSKIE HAS GONE on to become the President and CEO of Outreach Realty Services, which is a successful full-service Real Estate Brokerage currently licensed in Connecticut, New York and soon in Georgia. Also, she is the President and CEO of the Outreach School of Real Estate. A Real Estate School licensed in Connecticut and eleven other reciprocal states. She is the managing member of MET Construction Management, which is now owned by her three children.

Last, but certainly not least, she is the Founder and Chieftain of the Ms. Millionaire Mindset Sisterhood, an International, faith-based sisterhood that is devoted to breaking the poverty curse over ourselves and the lives of our loved ones, creating generational wealth, building legacies, group economics, and working in unity. The women in the Millionaire Mindset Sisterhood are in constant pursuit of their Divine Purpose and their Divine Passions that create their Divine Prosperity. November 2017, her story of her being homelessness, and how she pays it forward by changing the life of a homeless man who returned her $10,000 check went viral and received national and international coverage. She was featured on ABC, NBC, CBS, NBC Nightly with Lester Holt, Japan TV, Telemundo network, CNN, Don Francisco Show, NY Times, Washington Post, and was even on the cover of newspapers in the country of Cyprus. The story went viral across the world, and the number of television networks and newspapers picking up her story was too vast to count.

Furthermore, she appointed Elmer, the homeless man who found her check, to her Board of Directors for the Outreach

Foundation and together they are combating poverty and homelessness by providing affordable housing, shelter, financial literacy, and home buying education to low and moderate-income families.

Through it all, the experience of a horrific childhood of poverty, Roberta discovered a pathway to freedom and millions of dollars. Roberta Hoskie is now a Real Estate guru and a powerful public speaker. She is also a Master Coach on Mindset, Real Estate, Wealth Creation, and How to Break the Poverty Curse. And now, she travels the world raising chapters of the Millionaire Mindset Sisterhood and helping people from all backgrounds Break the Curse of Poverty.

Your Destiny Is Bigger Than Your Past.